BEOWULF

AN ANGLO-SAXON EPIC POEM

Translated by
John Lesslie Hall

COLLINS
CLASSICS

Harper Press
An imprint of HarperCollins*Publishers*
77–85 Fulham Palace Road
Hammersmith
London W6 8JB

This Harper Press paperback edition published 2012

John Lesslie Hall asserts the moral right to be identified as the author of this work

A catalogue record for this book is available from the British Library

ISBN: 978-0-00-792540-7

Printed and bound in Great Britain by Clays Ltd, St Ives plc

MIX
Paper from
responsible sources
FSC www.fsc.org   FSC™ C007454

FSC™ is a non-profit international organisation established to promote the
responsible management of the world's forests. Products carrying the FSC label
are independently certified to assure consumers that they come
from forests that are managed to meet the social, economic and
ecological needs of present and future generations.

Find out more about HarperCollins and the environment at
www.harpercollins.co.uk/green

Life & Times section © HarperCollins*Publishers* Ltd
Gerard Cheshire asserts his moral rights as author of the Life & Times section
Classic Literature: Words and Phrases adapted from
Collins English Dictionary
Typesetting in Kalix by Palimpsest Book Production Limited,
Falkirk, Stirlingshire

Lines that were missing in the original transcription used by Hall are represented
by asterisks in the text.

10 9 8 7 6 5 4 3 2

History of Collins

In 1819, millworker William Collins from Glasgow, Scotland, set up a company for printing and publishing pamphlets, sermons, hymn books and prayer books. That company was Collins and was to mark the birth of HarperCollins Publishers as we know it today. The long tradition of Collins dictionary publishing can be traced back to the first dictionary William published in 1824, *Greek and English Lexicon*. Indeed, from 1840 onwards, he began to produce illustrated dictionaries and even obtained a licence to print and publish the Bible.

Soon after, William published the first Collins novel, *Ready Reckoner*; however, it was the time of the Long Depression, where harvests were poor, prices were high, potato crops had failed and violence was erupting in Europe. As a result, many factories across the country were forced to close down and William chose to retire in 1846, partly due to the hardships he was facing.

Aged 30, William's son, William II, took over the business. A keen humanitarian with a warm heart and a generous spirit, William II was truly 'Victorian' in his outlook. He introduced new, up-to-date steam presses and published affordable editions of Shakespeare's works and *The Pilgrim's Progress*, making them available to the masses for the first time. A new demand for educational books meant that success came with the publication of travel books, scientific books, encyclopaedias and dictionaries. This demand to be educated led to the later publication of atlases, and Collins also held the monopoly on scripture writing at the time.

In the 1860s Collins began to expand and diversify,

and the idea of 'books for the millions' was developed. Affordable editions of classical literature were published and in 1903 Collins introduced 10 titles in their Collins Handy Illustrated Pocket Novels. These proved so popular that a few years later this had increased to an output of 50 volumes, selling nearly half a million in their year of publication. In the same year, The Everyman's Library was also instituted, with the idea of publishing an affordable library of the most important classical works, biographies, religious and philosophical treatments, plays, poems, travel and adventure. This series eclipsed all competition at the time and the introduction of paperback books in the 1950s helped to open that market and marked a high point in the industry.

HarperCollins is and has always been a champion of the classics and the current Collins Classics series follows in this tradition – publishing classical literature that is affordable and available to all. Beautifully packaged, highly collectible and intended to be reread and enjoyed at every opportunity.

Life & Times

Fact or Fiction?

Beowulf is a narrative poem that has survived since the Anglo-Saxon period. The story is set in Scandinavia and has its origin in the Nordic or Viking invasion of Britain, preceding the Norman invasion at the turn of the first millennium, in 1066. The manuscript has been frequently referenced as a source of socio-cultural information about the British people at that time, because there is a dearth of historical documentation relating to that period. This was due to the historical significance of oral tradition, rather than written, so very little was actually recorded.

In 1936 the fantasy novelist J.R.R. Tolkien presented a paper entitled *Beowulf: The Monsters and the Critics*, promoting the historical and social study of *Beowulf* in the context of literary and artistic content, elements often overlooked. This is because the tale is filled with mythical content, such as giants and dragons, and literature deemed as fantasy tended to be disregarded by historians. The point Tolkien was making is that such details are actually entirely relevant to socio-cultural study because they serve to inform the reader about belief systems in Britain and Europe at that time.

Ironically, however, Tolkien shot himself in the foot with this thesis, as it highlighted the fact that his own work was based on fantasy, with nothing whatsoever to do with real belief systems, therefore creating a faux presentation of seemingly similar ideas. Unlike in Tolkein's world, monsters and myths to the Anglo-Saxons were not make-believe: they were perceived as real phenomena to be believed in and feared.

Belief in the supernatural, or preternatural, realm was part and parcel of the ubiquitous cosmology of humanity in the Dark Ages, so *Beowulf* was not intended as pure entertainment like *Lord of the Rings* or *The Hobbit*. It would have been considered a true account of the past by those who heard the story contemporaneous to it being written down. The reason why *Beowulf* comes across as entertainment in the modern age is partly because we have an informed view of the world, so that we now know that supernatural ideas are products of the imagination. But it is also because the work is evidence of the oral tradition at that time, so the story would have evolved into an enjoyable tale as it passed from one storyteller to the next. After all, an audience would still have needed its imagination captured for a story to be remembered, so that the meme survived through the generations.

The Nowell Codex

Of course, it is perfectly possible that many other tales were written down at the same time as *Beowulf*, but that *Beowulf* was the only one to survive the ravages of time. In point of fact, it is remarkable that any manuscript of such antiquity should have survived at all, given that the British climate is better suited to deterioration and decay than desiccation and preservation. The manuscript was also badly damaged by fire along the way, but somehow its cargo of words journeyed from the Dark Ages, through the Middle Ages and into the Modern Age. As a result, *Beowulf* is a unique and significant artefact.

Beowulf was also written anonymously, adding an element of mystery and intrigue. As relatively few people could read and write at that time, or had the time and opportunity to learn to be literate, the story was most probably written down by a monk or someone else with academic inclination.

The manuscript itself is known as the Nowell Codex and contains a number of other documents in addition to *Beowulf*. It is written in Old English and is thought to date from around the 10th and early 11th centuries, which equates to the transition from the Early Medieval Period to the Middle Medieval Period. At that time, Old English was still in its archaic form, having absorbed some Norse influence, but was yet to be influenced by the Franconian tongue of the Normans, which led to Middle English. This evolution of language is what linguists use to date written documents lacking provenance. This is described as linguachronology. Although Old English is the basis for Modern English, it is fair to say that the two are substantially different in form and vocabulary, so contemporary versions of *Beowulf* are effectively translations. More accurately, they are transliterations, so there is always a certain degree of interpretation in the choice of equivalent word, sentence, phrase and so on. This is especially true with poetry because it is required to maintain poetic form to avoid becoming prosaic so, in essence, only the story remains intact.

As Old English was limited in its vocabulary, the original *Beowulf* manuscript is written in alliterative poetry. This means that the poetic device is the repetition of vocal sounds, rather than the rhyme or syllabic structure we usually think of as poetry. It is, in fact, prosody, a sort of hybrid between prose and poetry.

Beowulf comprises 3,182 lines of alliterative verse, and this method of documenting the story may have been the choice of the author. It is likely that the story itself was related in any number of ways by the different storytellers of the time, but that the author took it upon himself to add some artistic license, because an epic poem carried more cachet as a literary work. This would also have presented a far greater and satisfying creative challenge to the author. Being literate was more than just being able to read and write – it was perceived as a gift bestowed upon the individual to use as a tool for lifting everyday language onto a higher plain. Consequently, the written word became something more special than simply recording information in the vernacular.

Suspending Disbelief

The story itself is a fairly straightforward tale of the character Beowulf around the 5th century, who is destined to become king of the Geats, a Swedish tribe. In the yarn, he does battle with a monster named Grendel, followed by an attack by Grendel's mother. Many years later he is confronted by a dragon. These three heroic trials are the key components of the work in establishing the legend of Beowulf, as they are used to demonstrate his fearlessness and strength as a leader of men.

Inevitably, literary historians have taken it upon themselves to overanalyse the work for symbolism and allegory in their own quests to gain academic notability. While it may be true that the monsters and dragons loosely represent the threat of other tribes intent on conquest, for the most part the tale of *Beowulf* is a work of entertainment imbued with supernatural elements that reflect the belief systems of specific peoples. Life was generally difficult, so audiences enjoyed tales of heroes who survived conflict against the odds for the sake of protecting their people. In a world where tribes continually fought over territory and resources, there was constant uncertainty about the future. Add to the mix pagan superstitions and an unscientific view of the world, and the world in which *Beowulf* is set becomes one of supernatural possibility. Beowulf himself is possessed of supernatural or magical powers, too, but this is not fantasy, as everyone believed in such phenomena at the time the story was written down. This is the reason literary historians need to tread carefully in reading too much into the meaning behind such stories. Monsters and dragons were just monsters and dragons – they didn't need to represent anything else, because they were terrifying entities in their own right to minds who believed they existed.

It is important to remember to draw a distinction between the real thing and modern stories that mimic in the genre of fantasy, because the vital ingredient of belief makes all the difference. Tolkien and his ilk believed they were somehow continuing a tradition because they themselves entirely failed to see this very distinction. In truth, they were taking foreboding elements of real belief systems and bringing them back to life within cartoon realms of their own imagination. Ironically, the readers of such modern imitations have to suspend their *disbelief* in order to enter such worlds of fantasy; the original audiences of *Beowulf* actually *believed* every word.

Of course, all of this debate leads one to ask the question: did Beowulf actually exist as a living person? Just like many accounts of kings in post-Roman Europe, there is probably an element of truth to this, but we can never know for sure, precisely because there is no documentation or archaeological evidence to prove it. The likelihood is that Beowulf was indeed a leader of the Geats some centuries before the story was recorded, and over time the stories of his exploits became intertwined with supernatural elements to make the story of his life more extraordinary and entertaining. Because today we believe that those past kings were only ordinary men who found themselves in positions of power, they needed to be elevated in terms of their mental and physical attributes in order to cultivate mystique and authority among their people.

BEOWULF

To

My Wife

CONTENTS

Preface

The present work is a modest effort to reproduce approximately, in modern measures, the venerable epic, *Beowulf*. *Approximately*, I repeat; for a very close reproduction of Anglo-Saxon verse would, to a large extent, be prose to a modern ear.

The Heyne-Socin text and glossary have been closely followed. Occasionally a deviation has been made, but always for what seemed good and sufficient reason. The translator does not aim to be an editor. Once in a while, however, he has added a conjecture of his own to the emendations quoted from the criticisms of other students of the poem.

This work is addressed to two classes of readers. From both of these alike the translator begs sympathy and co-operation. The Anglo-Saxon scholar he hopes to please by adhering faithfully to the original. The student of English literature he aims to interest by giving him, in modern garb, the most ancient epic of our race. This is a bold and venturesome undertaking; and yet there must be some students of the Teutonic past willing to follow even a daring guide, if they may read in modern phrases of the sorrows of Hrothgar, of the prowess of Beowulf, and of the feelings that stirred the hearts of our forefathers in their primeval homes.

In order to please the larger class of readers, a regular cadence has been used, a measure which, while retaining the essential characteristics of the original, permits the reader to see ahead of him in reading.

Perhaps every Anglo-Saxon scholar has his own theory as to how *Beowulf* should be translated. Some have given us prose versions of what we believe to be a great poem. Is it any reflection on our honored Kemble and Arnold to say that their translations fail to show a layman that *Beowulf* is justly called our first *epic*? Of those translators who have used verse, several have written from what would seem a mistaken point of view. Is it proper, for instance, that the grave and solemn speeches of Beowulf and Hrothgar be put in ballad measures, tripping lightly and airily along? Or, again, is it fitting that the rough martial music of Anglo-Saxon verse be interpreted to us in the smooth measures of modern blank verse? Do we hear what has been beautifully called 'the clanging tread of a warrior in mail'?

Of all English translations of *Beowulf*, that of Professor Garnett alone gives any adequate idea of the chief characteristics of this great Teutonic epic.

The measure used in the present translation is believed to be as near a reproduction of the original as modern English affords. The cadences closely resemble those used by Browning in some of his most striking poems. The four stresses of the Anglo-Saxon verse are retained, and as much thesis and anacrusis is allowed as is consistent with a regular cadence. Alliteration has been used to a large extent; but it was thought that modern ears would hardly tolerate it on every line. End-rhyme has been used occasionally; internal rhyme, sporadically. Both have some warrant in Anglo-Saxon poetry. (For end-rhyme, see 1 53, 1 54; for internal rhyme, 2 21, 6 40.)

What Gummere[1] calls the 'rime-giver' has been studiously kept; *viz.*, the first accented syllable in the second half-verse always carries the alliteration; and the last accented syllable alliterates only sporadically. Alternate alliteration is occasionally used as in the original. (See 7 61, 8 5.)

No two accented syllables have been brought together, except occasionally after a cæsural pause. (See 2 19 and 12 1.) Or, scientifically speaking, Sievers's C type has been avoided as not consonant with the plan of translation. Several of his types, however, constantly occur; *e.g.* A and a variant (/ x | / x) (/ x x | / x); B and a variant (x / | x /) (x x / | x /); a variant of D (/ x | / x x); E (/ x x | /). Anacrusis gives further variety to the types used in the translation.

The parallelisms of the original have been faithfully preserved. (*E.g.*, 1 16 and 1 17: 'Lord' and 'Wielder of Glory'; 1 30, 1 31, 1 32; 2 12 and 2 13; 2 27 and 2 28; 3 5 and 3 6.) Occasionally, some loss has been sustained; but, on the other hand, a gain has here and there been made.

The effort has been made to give a decided flavor of archaism to the translation. All words not in keeping with the spirit of the poem have been avoided. Again, though many archaic words have been used, there are none, it is believed, which are not found in standard modern poetry.

---

[1] Handbook of Poetics, page 175, 1st edition.

Abbreviations Used in the Notes

B. = Bugge. C. = Cosijn. Gr. = Grein. Grdvtg. = Grundtvig.
H. = Heyne. H. and S. = Harrison and Sharp. H.-So. = Heyne-
Socin. K.= Kemble. Kl. = Kluge. M.= Müllenhoff. R. = Rieger.
S. = Sievers. Sw. = Sweet. t.B. = ten Brink. Th. = Thorpe.
W. = Wülcker.

Glossary of Proper Names

[The figures refer to the divisions of the poem in which the respective names occur. The bold figures refer to fitts, the roman, to lines in the fitts.]

Ælfhere.—A kinsman of Wiglaf.—36 3.

Æschere.—Confidential friend of King Hrothgar. Elder brother of Yrmenlaf. Killed by Grendel.—21 3; 30 89.

Beanstan.—Father of Breca.—9 26.

Beowulf.—Son of Scyld, the founder of the dynasty of Scyldings. Father of Healfdene, and grandfather of Hrothgar.—1 18; 2 1.

Beowulf.—The hero of the poem. Sprung from the stock of Geats, son of Ecgtheow. Brought up by his maternal grandfather Hrethel, and figuring in manhood as a devoted liegeman of his uncle Higelac. A hero from his youth. Has the strength of thirty men. Engages in a swimming-match with Breca. Goes to the help of Hrothgar against the monster Grendel. Vanquishes Grendel and his mother. Afterwards becomes king of the Geats. Late in life attempts to kill a fire-spewing dragon, and is slain. Is buried with great honors. His memorial mound.—6 26; 7 2; 7 9; 9 3; 9 8; 12 28; 12 43; 23 1, etc.

Breca.—Beowulf's opponent in the famous swimming-match.—9 8; 9 19; 9 21; 9 22.

Brondings.—A people ruled by Breca.—9 23.

Brosinga mene.—A famous collar once owned by the Brosings.—19 7.

Cain.—Progenitor of Grendel and other monsters.—2 56; 20 11.

Dæghrefn.—A warrior of the Hugs, killed by Beowulf.—35 40.

Danes.—Subjects of Scyld and his descendants, and hence often called Scyldings. Other names for them are Victory-Scyldings, Honor-Scyldings, Armor-Danes, Bright-Danes, East-Danes, West-Danes, North-Danes, South-Danes, Ingwins, Hrethmen.—1 1; 2 1; 3 2; 5 14; 7 1, etc.

Ecglaf.—Father of Unferth, who taunts Beowulf.—9 1.

Ecgtheow.—Father of Beowulf, the hero of the poem. A widely-known Wægmunding warrior. Marries Hrethel's daughter. After slaying Heatholaf, a Wylfing, he flees his country.—7 3; 5 6; 8 4.

Ecgwela.—A king of the Danes before Scyld.—25 60.

Elan.—Sister of Hrothgar, and probably wife of Ongentheow, king of the Swedes.—2 10.

Eagle Cape.—A promontory in Geat-land, under which took place Beowulf's last encounter.—41 87.

Eadgils.—Son of Ohthere and brother of Eanmund.—34 2.

Eanmund.—Son of Ohthere and brother of Eadgils. The reference to these brothers is vague, and variously understood. Heyne supposes as follows: Raising a revolt against their father, they are obliged to leave Sweden. They go to the land of the Geats; with what intention, is not known, but probably to conquer and plunder. The Geatish king, Heardred, is slain by one of the brothers, probably Eanmund.—36 10; 31 54 to 31 60; 33 66 to 34 6.

Eofor.—A Geatish hero who slays Ongentheow in war, and is rewarded by Hygelac with the hand of his only daughter.—41 18; 41 48.

Eormenric.—A Gothic king, from whom Hama took away the famous Brosinga mene.—19 9.

Eomær.—Son of Offa and Thrytho, king and queen of the Angles.—28 69.

Finn.—King of the North-Frisians and the Jutes. Marries Hildeburg. At his court takes place the horrible slaughter in which the Danish general, Hnæf, fell. Later on, Finn himself is slain by Danish warriors.—17 18; 17 30; 17 44; 18 4; 18 23.

Fin-land.—The country to which Beowulf was driven by the currents in his swimming-match.—10 22.

Fitela.—Son and nephew of King Sigemund, whose praises are sung in XIV.—14 42; 14 53.

Folcwalda.—Father of Finn.—17 38.

Franks.—Introduced occasionally in referring to the death of Higelac.—19 19; 40 21; 40 24.

Frisians.—A part of them are ruled by Finn. Some of them were engaged in the struggle in which Higelac was slain.—17 20; 17 42; 17 52; 40 21.

Freaware.—Daughter of King Hrothgar. Married to Ingeld, a Heathobard prince.—29 60; 30 32.

Froda.—King of the Heathobards, and father of Ingeld.—29 62.

Garmund.—Father of Offa.—28 71.

Geats, Geatmen.—The race to which the hero of the poem belongs. Also called Weder-Geats, or Weders, War-Geats, Sea-Geats. They are ruled by Hrethel, Hæthcyn, Higelac, and Beowulf.—4 7; 7 4; 10 45; 11 8; 27 14; 28 8.

Gepids.—Named in connection with the Danes and Swedes.—35 34.

Grendel.—A monster of the race of Cain. Dwells in the fens and moors. Is furiously envious when he hears sounds of joy in Hrothgar's palace. Causes the king untold agony for years. Is finally conquered by Beowulf, and dies of his wound. His hand and arm are hung up in Hrothgar's hall Heorot. His head is cut off by Beowulf when he goes down to fight with Grendel's mother.—2 50; 3 1; 3 13; 8 19; 11 17; 12 2; 13 27; 15 3.

Guthlaf.—A Dane of Hnæf's party.—18 24.

Half-Danes.—Branch of the Danes to which Hnæf belonged.—17 19.

Halga.—Surnamed the Good. Younger brother of Hrothgar.—2 9.

Hama.—Takes the Brosinga mene from Eormenric.—19 7.

Hæreth.—Father of Higelac's queen, Hygd.—28 39; 29 18.

Hæthcyn.—Son of Hrethel and brother of Higelac. Kills his brother Herebeald accidentally. Is slain at Ravenswood, fighting against Ongentheow.—34 43; 35 23; 40 32.

Helmings.—The race to which Queen Wealhtheow belonged.—10 63.

Heming.—A kinsman of Garmund, perhaps nephew.—28 54; 28 70.

Hengest.—A Danish leader. Takes command on the fall of Hnæf.—17 33; 17 41.

Herebeald.—Eldest son of Hrethel, the Geatish king, and brother of Higelac. Killed by his younger brother Hæthcyn.—34 43; 34 47.

Heremod.—A Danish king of a dynasty before the Scylding line. Was a source of great sorrow to his people.—14 64; 25 59.

Hereric.—Referred to as uncle of Heardred, but otherwise unknown.—31 60.

Hetwars.—Another name for the Franks.—33 51.

Healfdene.—Grandson of Scyld and father of Hrothgar. Ruled the Danes long and well.—2 5; 4 1; 8 14.

Heardred.—Son of Higelac and Hygd, king and queen of the Geats. Succeeds his father, with Beowulf as regent. Is slain by the sons of Ohthere.—31 56; 33 63; 33 75.

Heathobards.—Race of Lombards, of which Froda is king. After Froda falls in battle with the Danes, Ingeld, his son, marries Hrothgar's daughter, Freaware, in order to heal the feud.—30 1; 30 6.

Heatholaf.—A Wylfing warrior slain by Beowulf's father.—8 5.

Heathoremes.—The people on whose shores Breca is cast by the waves during his contest with Beowulf.—9 21.

Heorogar.—Elder brother of Hrothgar, and surnamed 'Weoroda Ræswa,' Prince of the Troopers.—2 9; 8 12.

Hereward.—Son of the above.—31 17.

Heort, Heorot.—The great mead-hall which King Hrothgar builds. It is invaded by Grendel for twelve years. Finally cleansed by Beowulf, the Geat. It is called Heort on account of the hart-antlers which decorate it.—2 25; 3 32; 3 52.

Hildeburg.—Wife of Finn, daughter of Hoce, and related to Hnæf,—probably his sister.—17 21; 18 34.

Hnæf.—Leader of a branch of the Danes called Half-Danes. Killed in the struggle at Finn's castle.—17 19; 17 61.

Hondscio.—One of Beowulf's companions. Killed by Grendel just before Beowulf grappled with that monster.—30 43.

Hoce.—Father of Hildeburg and probably of Hnæf.—17 26.

Hrethel.—King of the Geats, father of Higelac, and grandfather of Beowulf.—7 4; 34 39.

Hrethla.—Once used for Hrethel.—7 82.

Hrethmen.—Another name for the Danes.—7 73.

Hrethric.—Son of Hrothgar.—18 65; 27 19.

Hreosna-beorh.—A promontory in Geat-land, near which Ohthere's sons made plundering raids.—35 18.

Hrothgar.—The Danish king who built the hall Heort, but was long unable to enjoy it on account of Grendel's persecutions. Marries Wealhtheow, a Helming lady. Has two sons and a daughter. Is a typical Teutonic king, lavish of gifts. A devoted liegelord, as his lamentations over slain liegemen prove. Also very appreciative of kindness, as is shown by his loving gratitude to Beowulf.—2 9; 2 12; 4 1; 8 10; 15 1; etc., etc.

Hrothmund.—Son of Hrothgar.—18 65.

Hrothulf.—Probably a son of Halga, younger brother of

Hrothgar. Certainly on terms of close intimacy in Hrothgar's palace.—16 26; 18 57.

Hrunting.—Unferth's sword, lent to Beowulf.—22 71; 25 9.

Hugs.—A race in alliance with the Franks and Frisians at the time of Higelac's fall.—35 41.

Hun.—A Frisian warrior, probably general of the Hetwars. Gives Hengest a beautiful sword.—18 19.

Hunferth.—Sometimes used for Unferth.

Hygelac, Higelac.—King of the Geats, uncle and liegelord of Beowulf, the hero of the poem.—His second wife is the lovely Hygd, daughter of Hæreth. The son of their union is Heardred. Is slain in a war with the Hugs, Franks, and Frisians combined. Beowulf is regent, and afterwards king of the Geats.—4 6; 5 4; 28 34; 29 9; 29 21; 31 56.

Hygd.—Wife of Higelac, and daughter of Hæreth. There are some indications that she married Beowulf after she became a widow.—28 37.

Ingeld.—Son of the Heathobard king, Froda. Marries Hrothgar's daughter, Freaware, in order to reconcile the two peoples.—29 62; 30 32.

Ingwins.—Another name for the Danes.—16 52; 20 69.

Jutes.—Name sometimes applied to Finn's people.—17 22; 17 38; 18 17.

Lafing.—Name of a famous sword presented to Hengest by Hun.—18 19.

Merewing.—A Frankish king, probably engaged in the war in which Higelac was slain.—40 29.

Nægling.—Beowulf's sword.—36 76.

Offa.—King of the Angles, and son of Garmund. Marries the terrible Thrytho who is so strongly contrasted with Hygd.—28 59; 28 66.

Ohthere.—Son of Ongentheow, king of the Swedes. He is father of Eanmund and Eadgils.—40 35; 40 39.

Onela.—Brother of Ohthere.—36 15; 40 39.

Ongentheow.—King of Sweden, of the Scylfing dynasty.

Married, perhaps, Elan, daughter of Healfdene.—35 26; 41 16.

Oslaf.—A Dane of Hnæf's party.—18 24.

Ravenswood.—The forest near which Hæthcyn was slain.—40 31; 40 41.

Scefing.—Applied (1 4) to Scyld, and meaning 'son of Scef.'

Scyld.—Founder of the dynasty to which Hrothgar, his father, and grandfather belonged. He dies, and his body is put on a vessel, and set adrift. He goes from Daneland just as he had come to it—in a bark.—1 4; 1 19; 1 27.

Scyldings.—The descendants of Scyld. They are also called Honor-Scyldings, Victory-Scyldings, War-Scyldings, etc. (See 'Danes,' above.)—2 1; 7 1; 8 1.

Scylfings.—A Swedish royal line to which Wiglaf belonged.—36 2.

Sigemund.—Son of Wæls, and uncle and father of Fitela. His struggle with a dragon is related in connection with Beowulf's deeds of prowess.—14 38; 14 47.

Swerting.—Grandfather of Higelac, and father of Hrethel.—19 11.

Swedes.—People of Sweden, ruled by the Scylfings.—35 13.

Thrytho.—Wife of Offa, king of the Angles. Known for her fierce and unwomanly disposition. She is introduced as a contrast to the gentle Hygd, queen of Higelac.—28 42; 28 56.

Unferth.—Son of Ecglaf, and seemingly a confidential courtier of Hrothgar. Taunts Beowulf for having taken part in the swimming-match. Lends Beowulf his sword when he goes to look for Grendel's mother. In the MS. sometimes written *Hunferth.* 9 1; 18 41.

Wæls.—Father of Sigemund.—14 60.

Wægmunding.—A name occasionally applied to Wiglaf and Beowulf, and perhaps derived from a common ancestor, Wægmund.—36 6; 38 61.

Weders.—Another name for Geats or Wedergeats.

Wayland.—A fabulous smith mentioned in this poem and in other old Teutonic literature.—7 83.

Wendels.—The people of Wulfgar, Hrothgar's messenger and retainer. (Perhaps = Vandals.)—6 30.

Wealhtheow.—Wife of Hrothgar. Her queenly courtesy is well shown in the poem.—10 55.

Weohstan, or **Wihstan.**—A Wægmunding, and father of Wiglaf.—36 1.

Whale's Ness.—A prominent promontory, on which Beowulf's mound was built.—38 52; 42 76.

Wiglaf.—Son of Wihstan, and related to Beowulf. He remains faithful to Beowulf in the fatal struggle with the fire-drake. Would rather die than leave his lord in his dire emergency.—36 1; 36 3; 36 28.

Wonred.—Father of Wulf and Eofor.—41 20; 41 26.

Wulf.—Son of Wonred. Engaged in the battle between Higelac's and Ongentheow's forces, and had a hand-to-hand fight with Ongentheow himself. Ongentheow disables him, and is thereupon slain by Eofor.—41 19; 41 29.

Wulfgar.—Lord of the Wendels, and retainer of Hrothgar.—6 18; 6 30.

Wylfings.—A people to whom belonged Heatholaf, who was slain by Ecgtheow.—8 6; 8 16.

Yrmenlaf.—Younger brother of Æschere, the hero whose death grieved Hrothgar so deeply.—21 4.

List of Words and Phrases not in General Use

ATHELING.—Prince, nobleman.

BAIRN.—Son, child.

BARROW.—Mound, rounded hill, funeral-mound.

BATTLE-SARK.—Armor.

BEAKER.—Cup, drinking-vessel.

BEGEAR.—Prepare.

BIGHT.—Bay, sea.

BILL.—Sword.

BOSS.—Ornamental projection.

BRACTEATE.—A round ornament on a necklace.

BRAND.—Sword.

BURN.—Stream.

BURNIE.—Armor.

CARLE.—Man, hero.

EARL.—Nobleman, any brave man.

EKE.—Also.

EMPRISE.—Enterprise, undertaking.

ERST.—Formerly.

ERST-WORTHY.—Worthy for a long time past.

FAIN.—Glad.

FERRY.—Bear, carry.

FEY.—Fated, doomed.

FLOAT.—Vessel, ship.

FOIN.—To lunge (Shaks.).

GLORY OF KINGS.—God.

GREWSOME.—Cruel, fierce.

HEFT.—Handle, hilt; used by synecdoche for 'sword.'

HELM.—Helmet, protector.

HENCHMAN.—Retainer, vassal.

HIGHT.—Am (was) named.

HOLM.—Ocean, curved surface of the sea.

HIMSEEMED.—(It) seemed to him.

LIEF.—Dear, valued.

MERE.—Sea; in compounds, 'mere-ways,' 'mere-currents,' etc.

MICKLE.—Much.

NATHLESS.—Nevertheless.

NAZE.—Edge (nose).

NESS.—Edge.

NICKER.—Sea-beast.

QUIT, QUITE.—Requite.

RATHE.—Quickly.

REAVE.—Bereave, deprive.

SAIL-ROAD.—Sea.

SETTLE.—Seat, bench.

SKINKER.—One who pours.

SOOTHLY.—Truly.

SWINGE.—Stroke, blow.

TARGE, TARGET.—Shield.

THROUGHLY.—Thoroughly.

TOLD.—Counted.

UNCANNY.—Ill-featured, grizzly.

UNNETHE.—Difficult.

WAR-SPEED.—Success in war.

WEB.—Tapestry (that which is 'woven').

WEEDED.—Clad (cf. widow's weeds).

WEEN.—Suppose, imagine.

WEIRD.—Fate, Providence.

WHILOM.—At times, formerly, often.

WIELDER.—Ruler. Often used of God; also in compounds, as 'Wielder of Glory,' 'Wielder of Worship.'

WIGHT.—Creature.

WOLD.—Plane, extended surface.

WOT.—Knows.

YOUNKER.—Youth.

I.

The Life and Death of Scyld

The famous race of Spear-Danes.

Lo! the Spear-Danes' glory through splendid achievements
The folk-kings' former fame we have heard of,
How princes displayed then their prowess-in-battle.

Scyld, their mighty king, in honor of whom they are often
called Scyldings. He is the great-grandfather of Hrothgar,
so prominent in the poem.

Oft Scyld the Scefing from scathers in numbers
From many a people their mead-benches tore.   5
Since first he found him friendless and wretched,
The earl had had terror: comfort he got for it,
Waxed 'neath the welkin, world-honor gained,
Till all his neighbors o'er sea were compelled to
Bow to his bidding and bring him their tribute: 10
An excellent atheling! After was borne him

A son is born to him, who receives the name of Beowulf—a
name afterwards made so famous by the hero of the poem.

A son and heir, young in his dwelling,
Whom God-Father sent to solace the people.
He had marked the misery malice had caused them,

¹That reaved of their rulers they wretched had erstwhile² 15
Long been afflicted. The Lord, in requital,
Wielder of Glory, with world-honor blessed him.
Famed was Beowulf, far spread the glory
Of Scyld's great son in the lands of the Danemen.

> The ideal Teutonic king lavishes gifts on his vassals.

So the carle that is young, by kindnesses rendered 20
The friends of his father, with fees in abundance
Must be able to earn that when age approacheth
Eager companions aid him requitingly,
When war assaults him serve him as liegemen:
By praise-worthy actions must honor be got 25
'Mong all of the races. At the hour that was fated

> Scyld dies at the hour appointed by Fate.

Scyld then departed to the All-Father's keeping
Warlike to wend him; away then they bare him
To the flood of the current, his fond-loving comrades,
As himself he had bidden, while the friend of the Scyldings 30
Word-sway wielded, and the well-lovèd land-prince
Long did rule them.³ The ring-stemmèd vessel,
Bark of the atheling, lay there at anchor,
Icy in glimmer and eager for sailing;

> By his own request, his body is laid on a vessel and wafted
> seaward.

---

¹ For the 'Þæt' of verse 15, Sievers suggests 'Þá' (= which). If this be accepted, the sentence 'He had . . . afflicted' will read: *He (i.e. God) had perceived the malice-caused sorrow which they, lordless, had formerly long endured.*

² For 'aldor-léase' (15) Gr. suggested 'aldor-ceare': *He perceived their distress, that they formerly had suffered life-sorrow a long while.*

³ A very difficult passage. 'Áhte' (31) has no object. H. supplies 'geweald' from the context; and our translation is based upon this assumption, though it is far from satisfactory. Kl. suggests 'lændagas' for 'lange': *And the beloved land-prince enjoyed (had) his transitory days (i.e. lived).* B. suggests a dislocation; but this is a dangerous doctrine, pushed rather far by that eminent scholar.

The belovèd leader laid they down there,   35
Giver of rings, on the breast of the vessel,
The famed by the mainmast. A many of jewels,
Of fretted embossings, from far-lands brought over,
Was placed near at hand then; and heard I not ever
That a folk ever furnished a float more superbly   40
With weapons of warfare, weeds for the battle,
Bills and burnies; on his bosom sparkled
Many a jewel that with him must travel
On the flush of the flood afar on the current.
And favors no fewer they furnished him soothly,   45
Excellent folk-gems, than others had given him
     He leaves Daneland on the breast of a bark.
Who when first he was born outward did send him
Lone on the main, the merest of infants:
And a gold-fashioned standard they stretched under
     heaven
High o'er his head, let the holm-currents bear him,   50
Seaward consigned him: sad was their spirit,
Their mood very mournful. Men are not able
     No one knows whither the boat drifted.
Soothly to tell us, they in halls who reside,[4]
Heroes under heaven, to what haven he hied.

[4] The reading of the H.-So. text has been quite closely followed; but some eminent scholars read 'séle-rædenne' for 'sele-rædende.' If that be adopted, the passage will read: *Men cannot tell us, indeed, the order of Fate, etc.* 'Sele-rædende' has two things to support it: (1) v. 1347; (2) it affords a parallel to 'men' in v. 50.

II.

Scyld's Successors—Hrothgar's Great Mead-Hall

Beowulf succeeds his father Scyld

In the boroughs then Beowulf, bairn of the Scyldings,
Belovèd land-prince, for long-lasting season
Was famed mid the folk (his father departed,
The prince from his dwelling), till afterward sprang
Great-minded Healfdene; the Danes in his lifetime   5
He graciously governed, grim-mooded, agèd.

Healfdene's birth.

Four bairns of his body born in succession
Woke in the world, war-troopers' leader
Heorogar, Hrothgar, and Halga the good;
Heard I that Elan was Ongentheow's consort,   10

He has three sons—one of them, Hrothgar—and a daughter
named Elan. Hrothgar becomes a mighty king.

The well-beloved bedmate of the War-Scylfing leader.
Then glory in battle to Hrothgar was given,
Waxing of war-fame, that willingly kinsmen
Obeyed his bidding, till the boys grew to manhood,
A numerous band. It burned in his spirit   15
To urge his folk to found a great building,
A mead-hall grander than men of the era

4

> He is eager to build a great hall in which he may feast his
> retainers

Ever had heard of, and in it to share
With young and old all of the blessings
The Lord had allowed him, save life and retainers.   20
Then the work I find afar was assigned
To many races in middle-earth's regions,
To adorn the great folk-hall. In due time it happened
Early 'mong men, that 'twas finished entirely,
The greatest of hall-buildings; Heorot he named it   25

> The hall is completed, and is called Heort, or Heorot.

Who wide-reaching word-sway wielded 'mong earlmen.
His promise he brake not, rings he lavished,
Treasure at banquet. Towered the hall up
High and horn-crested, huge between antlers:
It battle-waves bided, the blasting fire-demon;   30
Ere long then from hottest hatred must sword-wrath
Arise for a woman's husband and father.
Then the mighty war-spirit[1] endured for a season,

> The Monster Grendel is madly envious of the Danemen's
> joy.

Bore it bitterly, he who bided in darkness,
That light-hearted laughter loud in the building   35
Greeted him daily; there was dulcet harp-music,
Clear song of the singer. He said that was able

> [The course of the story is interrupted by a short reference
> to some old account of the creation.]

To tell from of old earthmen's beginnings,
That Father Almighty earth had created,
The winsome wold that the water encircleth,   40
Set exultingly the sun's and the moon's beams
To lavish their lustre on land-folk and races,

---

[1] R. and t. B. prefer 'ellor-gæst' to 'ellen-gæst' (86): *Then the stranger from
afar endured, etc.*

And earth He embellished in all her regions
With limbs and leaves; life He bestowed too
On all the kindreds that live under heaven. 45

The glee of the warriors is overcast by a horrible dread.

So blessed with abundance, brimming with joyance,
The warriors abided, till a certain one gan to
Dog them with deeds of direfullest malice,
A foe in the hall-building: this horrible stranger[2]
Was Grendel entitled, the march-stepper famous 50
Who[3] dwelt in the moor-fens, the marsh and
the fastness;
The wan-mooded being abode for a season
In the land of the giants, when the Lord and Creator
Had banned him and branded. For that bitter murder,
The killing of Abel, all-ruling Father 55

Cain is referred to as a progenitor of Grendel, and of
monsters in general.

The kindred of Cain crushed with His vengeance;
In the feud He rejoiced not, but far away drove him
From kindred and kind, that crime to atone for,
Meter of Justice. Thence ill-favored creatures,
Elves and giants, monsters of ocean, 60
Came into being, and the giants that longtime
Grappled with God; He gave them requital.

---

[2] Some authorities would translate '*demon*' instead of '*stranger*.'
[3] Some authorities arrange differently, and render: *Who dwelt in the moor-fens, the marsh and the fastness, the land of the giant-race.*

III.

Grendel the Murderer

Grendel attacks the sleeping heroes
When the sun was sunken, he set out to visit
The lofty hall-building, how the Ring-Danes had used it
For beds and benches when the banquet was over.
Then he found there reposing many a noble
Asleep after supper; sorrow the heroes,[1]   5
Misery knew not. The monster of evil
Greedy and cruel tarried but little,
    He drags off thirty of them, and devours them
Fell and frantic, and forced from their slumbers
Thirty of thanemen; thence he departed
Leaping and laughing, his lair to return to,   10
With surfeit of slaughter sallying homeward.
In the dusk of the dawning, as the day was just breaking,
Was Grendel's prowess revealed to the warriors:
    A cry of agony goes up, when Grendel's horrible deed is
    fully realized.
Then, his meal-taking finished, a moan was uplifted,

---

[1] The translation is based on 'weras,' adopted by H.-So.—K. and Th. read
'wera' and, arranging differently, render 119(2)—120: *They knew not sorrow,
the wretchedness of man, aught of misfortune.*—For 'unhælo' (120) R. suggests
'unfælo': *The uncanny creature, greedy and cruel, etc.*

Morning-cry mighty. The man-ruler famous,   15
The long-worthy atheling, sat very woful,
Suffered great sorrow, sighed for his liegemen,
When they had seen the track of the hateful pursuer,
The spirit accursèd: too crushing that sorrow,
> The monster returns the next night.

Too loathsome and lasting. Not longer he tarried,   20
But one night after continued his slaughter
Shameless and shocking, shrinking but little
From malice and murder; they mastered him fully.
He was easy to find then who otherwhere looked for
A pleasanter place of repose in the lodges,   25
A bed in the bowers. Then was brought to his notice
Told him truly by token apparent
The hall-thane's hatred: he held himself after
Further and faster who the foeman did baffle.
[2]So ruled he and strongly strove against justice   30
Lone against all men, till empty uptowered
> King Hrothgar's agony and suspense last twelve years.

The choicest of houses. Long was the season:
Twelve-winters' time torture suffered
The friend of the Scyldings, every affliction,
Endless agony; hence it after[3] became   35
Certainly known to the children of men
Sadly in measures, that long against Hrothgar
Grendel struggled:—his grudges he cherished,
Murderous malice, many a winter,
Strife unremitting, and peacefully wished he   40

---

[2] S. rearranges and translates: *So he ruled and struggled unjustly, one against all, till the noblest of buildings stood useless (it was a long while) twelve years' time: the friend of the Scyldings suffered distress, every woe, great sorrows, etc.*

[3] For 'syððan,' B. suggests 'sárcwidum': *Hence in mournful words it became well known, etc.* Various other words beginning with 's' have been conjectured.

[4]Life-woe to lift from no liegeman at all of
The men of the Dane-folk, for money to settle,
No counsellor needed count for a moment
On handsome amends at the hands of the murderer;
  Grendel is unremitting in his persecutions.
The monster of evil fiercely did harass,   45
The ill-planning death-shade, both elder and younger,
Trapping and tricking them. He trod every night then
The mist-covered moor-fens; men do not know where
Witches and wizards wander and ramble.
So the foe of mankind many of evils   50
Grievous injuries, often accomplished,
Horrible hermit; Heort he frequented,
Gem-bedecked palace, when night-shades had fallen
  God is against the monster.
(Since God did oppose him, not the throne could he
  touch,[5]
The light-flashing jewel, love of Him knew not).   55
'Twas a fearful affliction to the friend of the Scyldings
  The king and his council deliberate in vain.
Soul-crushing sorrow. Not seldom in private
Sat the king in his council; conference held they
What the braves should determine 'gainst terrors
  unlooked for.

---

[4] The H.-So. glossary is very inconsistent in referring to this passage.—
'Sibbe' (154), which H.-So. regards as an instr., B. takes as accus., obj. of
'wolde.' Putting a comma after Deniga, he renders: *He did not desire peace
with any of the Danes, nor did he wish to remove their life-woe, nor to settle
for money.*
[5] Of this difficult passage the following interpretations among others are
given: (1) Though Grendel has frequented Heorot as a demon, he could
not become ruler of the Danes, on account of his hostility to God.
(2) Hrothgar was much grieved that Grendel had not appeared before his
throne to receive presents. (3) He was not permitted to devastate the hall,
on account of the Creator; *i.e.* God wished to make his visit fatal to him.—
Ne . . . wisse (169) W. renders: *Nor had he any desire to do so*; 'his' being
obj. gen. = danach.

They invoke the aid of their gods.

At the shrines of their idols often they promised   60
Gifts and offerings, earnestly prayed they
The devil from hell would help them to lighten
Their people's oppression. Such practice they used then,
Hope of the heathen; hell they remembered
In innermost spirit, God they knew not,   65

The true God they do not know.

Judge of their actions, All-wielding Ruler,
No praise could they give the Guardian of Heaven,
The Wielder of Glory. Woe will be his who
Through furious hatred his spirit shall drive to
The clutch of the fire, no comfort shall look for,   70
Wax no wiser; well for the man who,
Living his life-days, his Lord may face
And find defence in his Father's embrace!

IV.

Beowulf Goes to Hrothgar's Assistance

Hrothgar sees no way of escape from the persecutions of
Grendel.

So Healfdene's kinsman constantly mused on
His long-lasting sorrow; the battle-thane clever
Was not anywise able evils to 'scape from:
Too crushing the sorrow that came to the people,
Loathsome and lasting the life-grinding torture,   5

Beowulf, the Geat, hero of the poem, hears of Hrothgar's
sorrow, and resolves to go to his assistance.

Greatest of night-woes. So Higelac's liegeman,
Good amid Geatmen, of Grendel's achievements
Heard in his home:[1] of heroes then living
He was stoutest and strongest, sturdy and noble.
He bade them prepare him a bark that was trusty;   10
He said he the war-king would seek o'er the ocean,
The folk-leader noble, since he needed retainers.
For the perilous project prudent companions

---

[1] 'From hám' (194) is much disputed. One rendering is: *Beowulf, being
away from home, heard of Hrothgar's troubles, etc.* Another, that adopted
by S. and endorsed in the H.-So. notes, is: *B. heard from his neighborhood
(neighbors),* i.e. *in his home, etc.* A third is: *B., being at home, heard this as
occurring away from home.* The H.-So. glossary and notes conflict.

Chided him little, though loving him dearly;
They egged the brave atheling, augured him glory.   15

> With fourteen carefully chosen companions, he sets out for
> Dane-land.

The excellent knight from the folk of the Geatmen
Had liegemen selected, likest to prove them
Trustworthy warriors; with fourteen companions
The vessel he looked for; a liegeman then showed them,
A sea-crafty man, the bounds of the country.   20
Fast the days fleeted; the float was a-water,
The craft by the cliff. Clomb to the prow then
Well-equipped warriors: the wave-currents twisted
The sea on the sand; soldiers then carried
On the breast of the vessel bright-shining jewels,   25
Handsome war-armor; heroes outshoved then,
Warmen the wood-ship, on its wished-for adventure.

> The vessel sails like a bird

The foamy-necked floater fanned by the breeze,
Likest a bird, glided the waters,

> In twenty four hours they reach the shores of Hrothgar's
> dominions

Till twenty and four hours thereafter   30
The twist-stemmed vessel had traveled such distance
That the sailing-men saw the sloping embankments,
The sea cliffs gleaming, precipitous mountains,
Nesses enormous: they were nearing the limits
At the end of the ocean.[2] Up thence quickly   35
The men of the Weders clomb to the mainland,
Fastened their vessel (battle weeds rattled,
War burnies clattered), the Wielder they thanked
That the ways o'er the waters had waxen so gentle.

---

[2] 'Eoletes' (224) is marked with a (?) by H.-So.; our rendering simply
follows his conjecture.—Other conjectures as to 'eolet' are: (1) *voyage*, (2)
toil, labor, (3) *hasty journey*.

They are hailed by the Danish coast guard

Then well from the cliff edge the guard of the Scyldings 40
Who the sea-cliffs should see to, saw o'er the gangway
Brave ones bearing beauteous targets,
Armor all ready, anxiously thought he,
Musing and wondering what men were approaching.   45
High on his horse then Hrothgar's retainer   50
Turned him to coastward, mightily brandished
His lance in his hands, questioned with boldness.

His challenge

'Who are ye men here, mail-covered warriors
Clad in your corslets, come thus a-driving
A high riding ship o'er the shoals of the waters,
³And hither 'neath helmets have hied o'er the ocean?
I have been strand-guard, standing as warden,
Lest enemies ever anywise ravage
Danish dominions with army of war-ships.
More boldly never have warriors ventured   55
Hither to come; of kinsmen's approval,
Word-leave of warriors, I ween that ye surely

He is struck by Beowulf's appearance.

Nothing have known. Never a greater one
Of earls o'er the earth have *I* had a sight of
Than is one of your number, a hero in armor;   60

---

³ The lacuna of the MS at this point has been supplied by various conjectures. The reading adopted by H.-So. has been rendered in the above translation. W., like H.-So., makes 'ic' the beginning of a new sentence, but, for 'helmas bæron,' he reads 'hringed stefnan.' This has the advantage of giving a parallel to 'brontne ceol' instead of a kenning for 'go.'—B puts the (?) after 'holmas', and begins a new sentence at the middle of the line. Translate: *What warriors are ye, clad in armor, who have thus come bringing the foaming vessel over the water way, hither over the seas? For some time on the wall I have been coast guard, etc.* S. endorses most of what B. says, but leaves out 'on the wall' in the last sentence. If W.'s 'hringed stefnan' be accepted, change line 51 above to, *A ring-stemmed vessel hither o'ersea.*

No low-ranking fellow[4] adorned with his weapons,
But launching them little, unless looks are deceiving,
And striking appearance. Ere ye pass on your journey
As treacherous spies to the land of the Scyldings
And farther fare, I fully must know now   65
What race ye belong to. Ye far-away dwellers,
Sea-faring sailors, my simple opinion
Hear ye and hearken: haste is most fitting
Plainly to tell me what place ye are come from.'

[4] 'Seld-guma' (249) is variously rendered: (1) *housecarle*; (2) *home-stayer*;
(3) *common man*. Dr. H. Wood suggests *a man-at-arms in another's house*.

V.

The Geats Reach Heorot

Beowulf courteously replies.

The chief of the strangers rendered him answer,
War-troopers' leader, and word-treasure opened:

We are Geats.

'We are sprung from the lineage of the people of
Geatland,
And Higelac's hearth-friends. To heroes unnumbered

My father Ecgtheow was well-known in his day.

My father was known, a noble head-warrior   5
Ecgtheow titled; many a winter
He lived with the people, ere he passed on his journey,
Old from his dwelling; each of the counsellors
Widely mid world-folk well remembers him.

Our intentions towards King Hrothgar are of the kindest.

We, kindly of spirit, the lord of thy people,   10
The son of King Healfdene, have come here to visit,
Folk-troop's defender: be free in thy counsels!
To the noble one bear we a weighty commission,
The helm of the Danemen; we shall hide, I ween,

Is it true that a monster is slaying Danish heroes?

Naught of our message. Thou know'st if it happen,   15
As we soothly heard say, that some savage despoiler,

Some hidden pursuer, on nights that are murky
By deeds very direful 'mid the Danemen exhibits
Hatred unheard of, horrid destruction
And the falling of dead. From feelings least selfish   20

> I can help your king to free himself from this horrible creature.

I am able to render counsel to Hrothgar,
How he, wise and worthy, may worst the destroyer,
If the anguish of sorrow should ever be lessened,[1]
Comfort come to him, and care-waves grow cooler,
Or ever hereafter he agony suffer   25
And troublous distress, while towereth upward
The handsomest of houses high on the summit.'

> The coast-guard reminds Beowulf that it is easier to say
> than to do.

Bestriding his stallion, the strand-watchman answered,
The doughty retainer: 'The difference surely
'Twixt words and works, the warlike shield-bearer   30
Who judgeth wisely well shall determine.
This band, I hear, beareth no malice

> I am satisfied of your good intentions, and shall lead you to
> the palace.

To the prince of the Scyldings. Pass ye then onward
With weapons and armor. I shall lead you in person;
To my war-trusty vassals command I shall issue   35
To keep from all injury your excellent vessel,

> Your boat shall be well cared for during your stay here.

Your fresh-tarred craft, 'gainst every opposer
Close by the sea-shore, till the curvèd-neckèd bark shall
Waft back again the well-beloved hero
O'er the way of the water to Weder dominions.   40

> He again compliments Beowulf.

---

[1] 'Edwendan' (280) B. takes to be the subs. 'edwenden' (cf. 1775); and
'bisigu' he takes as gen. sing., limiting 'edwenden': *If reparation for sorrows
is ever to come.* This is supported by t.B.

To warrior so great 'twill be granted sure
In the storm of strife to stand secure.'
Onward they fared then (the vessel lay quiet,
The broad-bosomed bark was bound by its cable,
Firmly at anchor); the boar-signs glistened[2]   45
Bright on the visors vivid with gilding,
Blaze-hardened, brilliant; the boar acted warden.
The heroes hastened, hurried the liegemen,

> The land is perhaps rolling.

Descended together, till they saw the great palace,
The well-fashioned wassail-hall wondrous and gleaming: 50

> Heorot flashes on their view.

'Mid world-folk and kindreds that was widest reputed
Of halls under heaven which the hero abode in;
Its lustre enlightened lands without number.
Then the battle-brave hero showed them the glittering
Court of the bold ones, that they easily thither   55
Might fare on their journey; the aforementioned warrior
Turning his courser, quoth as he left them:

> The coast-guard, having discharged his duty, bids them
> God-speed.

''Tis time I were faring; Father Almighty
Grant you His grace, and give you to journey
Safe on your mission! To the sea I will get me   60
'Gainst hostile warriors as warden to stand.'

---

[2] Combining the emendations of B. and t.B., we may read: *The boar-images glistened . . . brilliant, protected the life of the war-mooded man.* They read 'ferh-wearde' (305) and 'gúðmódgum men' (306).

VI.

Beowulf Introduces Himself at the Palace

The highway glistened with many-hued pebble,
A by-path led the liegemen together.
[1]Firm and hand-locked the war-burnie glistened,
The ring-sword radiant rang 'mid the armor
As the party was approaching the palace together   5

> They set their arms and armor against the wall.

In warlike equipments. 'Gainst the wall of the building
Their wide-fashioned war-shields they weary did set then,
Battle-shields sturdy; benchward they turned then;
Their battle-sarks rattled, the gear of the heroes;
The lances stood up then, all in a cluster,   10
The arms of the seamen, ashen-shafts mounted
With edges of iron: the armor-clad troopers

> A Danish hero asks them whence and why they are come.

Were decked with weapons. Then a proud-mooded hero
Asked of the champions questions of lineage:
'From what borders bear ye your battle-shields plated,   15
Gilded and gleaming, your gray-colored burnies,

---

[1] Instead of the punctuation given by H.-So, S. proposed to insert a comma
after 'scír' (322), and to take 'hring-íren' as meaning 'ring-mail' and as
parallel with 'gúð-byrne.' The passage would then read: *The firm and
hand-locked war-burnie shone, bright ring-mail, rang 'mid the armor, etc.*

Helmets with visors and heap of war-lances?—
To Hrothgar the king I am servant and liegeman.
'Mong folk from far-lands found I have never

He expresses no little admiration for the strangers.

Men so many of mien more courageous.   20
I ween that from valor, nowise as outlaws,
But from greatness of soul ye sought for King Hrothgar.'

Beowulf replies.

Then the strength-famous earlman answer rendered,
The proud-mooded Wederchief replied to his question,

We are Higelac's table-companions, and bear an important
commission to your prince.

Hardy 'neath helmet: 'Higelac's mates are we;   25
Beowulf hight I. To the bairn of Healfdene,
The famous folk-leader, I freely will tell
To thy prince my commission, if pleasantly hearing
He'll grant we may greet him so gracious to all men.'
Wulfgar replied then (he was prince of the Wendels,   30
His boldness of spirit was known unto many,
His prowess and prudence): 'The prince of the Scyldings,

Wulfgar, the thane, says that he will go and ask Hrothgar
whether he will see the strangers.

The friend-lord of Danemen, I will ask of thy journey,
The giver of rings, as thou urgest me do it,
The folk-chief famous, and inform thee early   35
What answer the good one mindeth to render me.'
He turned then hurriedly where Hrothgar was sitting,
²Old and hoary, his earlmen attending him;
The strength-famous went till he stood at the shoulder
Of the lord of the Danemen, of courteous thanemen   40
The custom he minded. Wulfgar addressed then
His friendly liegelord: 'Folk of the Geatmen

---

² Gr. and others translate 'unhár' by 'bald'; *old and bald*.

> He thereupon urges his liegelord to receive the visitors
> courteously.

O'er the way of the waters are wafted hither,
Faring from far-lands: the foremost in rank
The battle-champions Beowulf title.   45
They make this petition: with thee, O my chieftain,
To be granted a conference; O gracious King Hrothgar,
Friendly answer refuse not to give them!

> Hrothgar, too, is struck with Beowulf's appearance.

In war-trappings weeded worthy they seem
Of earls to be honored; sure the atheling is doughty   50
Who headed the heroes hitherward coming.'

VII.

Hrothgar and Beowulf

Hrothgar remembers Beowulf as a youth, and also
remembers his father.

Hrothgar answered, helm of the Scyldings:
'I remember this man as the merest of striplings.
His father long dead now was Ecgtheow titled,
Him Hrethel the Geatman granted at home his
One only daughter; his battle-brave son   5
Is come but now, sought a trustworthy friend.
Sea-faring sailors asserted it then,

Beowulf is reported to have the strength of thirty men.

Who valuable gift-gems of the Geatmen[1] carried
As peace-offering thither, that he thirty men's grapple
Has in his hand, the hero-in-battle.   10

God hath sent him to our rescue.

The holy Creator usward sent him,
To West-Dane warriors, I ween, for to render
'Gainst Grendel's grimness gracious assistance:
I shall give to the good one gift-gems for courage.

---

[1] Some render 'gif-sceattas' by 'tribute.'—'Géata' B. and Th. emended to
'Géatum.' If this be accepted, change 'of the Geatmen' to 'to the Geatmen.'

Hasten to bid them hither to speed them,[2]   15
To see assembled this circle of kinsmen;
Tell them expressly they're welcome in sooth to
The men of the Danes.' To the door of the building
> Wulfgar invites the strangers in.

Wulfgar went then, this word-message shouted:
'My victorious liegelord bade me to tell you,   20
The East-Danes' atheling, that your origin knows he,
And o'er wave-billows wafted ye welcome are hither,
Valiant of spirit. Ye straightway may enter
Clad in corslets, cased in your helmets,
To see King Hrothgar. Here let your battle-boards,   25
Wood-spears and war-shafts, await your conferring.'
The mighty one rose then, with many a liegeman,
An excellent thane-group; some there did await them,
And as bid of the brave one the battle-gear guarded.
Together they hied them, while the hero did
   guide them,   30
'Neath Heorot's roof; the high-minded went then
Sturdy 'neath helmet till he stood in the building.
Beowulf spake (his burnie did glisten,
His armor seamed over by the art of the craftsman):
> Beowulf salutes Hrothgar, and then proceeds to boast of his
> youthful achievements.

'Hail thou, Hrothgar! I am Higelac's kinsman   35
And vassal forsooth; many a wonder
I dared as a stripling. The doings of Grendel,
In far-off fatherland I fully did know of:
Sea-farers tell us, this hall-building standeth,
Excellent edifice, empty and useless   40
To all the earlmen after evenlight's glimmer

---

[2] If t.B.'s emendation of vv. 386, 387 be accepted, the two lines, 'Hasten
. . . kinsmen' will read: *Hasten thou, bid the throng of kinsmen go into the
hall together.*

'Neath heaven's bright hues hath hidden its glory.
This my earls then urged me, the most excellent
    of them,
Carles very clever, to come and assist thee,
Folk-leader Hrothgar; fully they knew of   45
      His fight with the nickers.
The strength of my body. Themselves they beheld me
When I came from the contest, when covered with
    gore
Foes I escaped from, where five[3] I had bound,
The giant-race wasted, in the waters destroying
The nickers by night, bore numberless sorrows,   50
The Weders avenged (woes had they suffered)
Enemies ravaged; alone now with Grendel
      He intends to fight Grendel unaided.
I shall manage the matter, with the monster of evil,
The giant, decide it. Thee I would therefore
Beg of thy bounty, Bright-Danish chieftain,   55
Lord of the Scyldings, this single petition:
Not to refuse me, defender of warriors,
Friend-lord of folks, so far have I sought thee,
That *I* may unaided, my earlmen assisting me,
This brave-mooded war-band, purify Heorot.   60
I have heard on inquiry, the horrible creature
      Since the monster uses no weapons,
From veriest rashness recks not for weapons;
I this do scorn then, so be Higelac gracious,

---

[3] For 420 (*b*) and 421 (*a*), B. suggests: Þær ic (on) fifelgeban ýðde eotena cyn = *where I in the ocean destroyed the eoten-race.*—t.B. accepts B.'s 'brilliant' 'fifelgeban,' omits 'on,' emends 'cyn' to 'hám,' arranging: Þær ic fifelgeban ýðde, eotena hám = *where I desolated the ocean, the home of the eotens.*—This would be better but for changing 'cyn' to 'hám.'—I suggest: Þær ic fifelgeband (cf. nhd. Bande) ýðde, eotena cyn = *where I conquered the monster band, the race of the eotens.* This makes no change except to read '*fifel*' for '*fife*.'

My liegelord belovèd, lenient of spirit,
To bear a blade or a broad-fashioned target,   65
A shield to the onset; only with hand-grip
>   I, too, shall disdain to use any.
The foe I must grapple, fight for my life then,
Foeman with foeman; he fain must rely on
The doom of the Lord whom death layeth hold of.
>   Should he crush me, he will eat my companions as he has
>   eaten thy thanes.
I ween he will wish, if he win in the struggle,   70
To eat in the war-hall earls of the Geat-folk,
Boldly to swallow[4] them, as of yore he did often
The best of the Hrethmen! Thou needest not trouble
A head-watch to give me;[5] he will have me dripping
>   In case of my defeat, thou wilt not have the trouble of
>   burying me.
And dreary with gore, if death overtake me,[6]   75
Will bear me off bleeding, biting and mouthing me,
The hermit will eat me, heedless of pity,
Marking the moor-fens; no more wilt thou need then
>   Should I fall, send my armor to my lord, King Higelac.

---

[4] 'Unforhte' (444) is much disputed.—H.-So. wavers between adj. and adv. Gr. and B. take it as an adv. modifying *etan: Will eat the Geats fearlessly.*— Kl. considers this reading absurd, and proposes 'anforhte' = timid.— Understanding 'unforhte' as an adj. has this advantage, viz. that it gives a parallel to 'Geátena leóde': but to take it as an adv. is more natural. Furthermore, to call the Geats 'brave' might, at this point, seem like an implied thrust at the Danes, so long helpless; while to call his own men 'timid' would be befouling his own nest.

[5] For 'head-watch,' cf. H.-So. notes and cf. v. 2910.—Th. translates: *Thou wilt not need my head to hide* (i.e., thou wilt have no occasion to bury me, as Grendel will devour me whole).—Simrock imagines a kind of dead-watch.—Dr. H. Wood suggests: *Thou wilt not have to bury so much as my head* (for Grendel will be a thorough undertaker),—grim humor.

[6] S. proposes a colon after 'nimeð' (l. 447). This would make no essential change in the translation.

Find me my food.[7] If I fall in the battle,
Send to Higelac the armor that serveth   80
To shield my bosom, the best of equipments,
Richest of ring-mails; 'tis the relic of Hrethla,
    Weird is supreme
The work of Wayland. Goes Weird as she must go!'

[7] Owing to the vagueness of 'feorme' (451), this passage is variously
translated. In our translation, H.-So.'s glossary has been quite closely
followed. This agrees substantially with B.'s translation (P. and B. XII. 87).
R. translates: *Thou needst not take care longer as to the consumption of my
dead body.* 'Líc' is also a crux here, as it may mean living body or dead
body.

VIII.

Hrothgar and Beowulf—*Continued*

Hrothgar responds.

Hrothgar discoursed, helm of the Scyldings:
'To defend our folk and to furnish assistance,[1]
Thou soughtest us hither, good friend Beowulf.

Reminiscences of Beowulf's father, Ecgtheow.

The fiercest of feuds thy father engaged in,
Heatholaf killed he in hand-to-hand conflict   5
'Mid Wilfingish warriors; then the Wederish people
For fear of a feud were forced to disown him.
Thence flying he fled to the folk of the South-Danes,
The race of the Scyldings, o'er the roll of the waters;
I had lately begun then to govern the Danemen,   10
The hoard-seat of heroes held in my youth,

---

[1] B. and S. reject the reading given in H.-So., and suggested by Grtvg. B.
suggests for 457–458:

> wáere-ryhtum Þú, wine mín Béowulf,
> and for ár-stafum úsic sóhtest.

This means: *From the obligations of clientage, my friend Beowulf, and for
assistance thou hast sought us.*—This gives coherence to Hrothgar's opening
remarks in VIII., and also introduces a new motive for Beowulf's coming
to Hrothgar's aid.

Rich in its jewels: dead was Heregar,
My kinsman and elder had earth-joys forsaken,
Healfdene his bairn. He was better than I am!
That feud thereafter for a fee I compounded;   15
O'er the weltering waters to the Wilfings I sent
Ornaments old; oaths did he swear me.

> Hrothgar recounts to Beowulf the horrors of Grendel's
> persecutions.

It pains me in spirit to any to tell it,
What grief in Heorot Grendel hath caused me,
What horror unlooked-for, by hatred unceasing.   20
Waned is my war-band, wasted my hall-troop;
Weird hath offcast them to the clutches of Grendel.
God can easily hinder the scather
From deeds so direful. Oft drunken with beer

> My thanes have made many boasts, but have not executed
> them.

O'er the ale-vessel promised warriors in armor   25
They would willingly wait on the wassailing-benches
A grapple with Grendel, with grimmest of edges.
Then this mead-hall at morning with murder was
        reeking,
The building was bloody at breaking of daylight,
The bench-deals all flooded, dripping and bloodied,   30
The folk-hall was gory: I had fewer retainers,
Dear-beloved warriors, whom death had laid hold of.

> Sit down to the feast, and give us comfort.

Sit at the feast now, thy intents unto heroes,[2]

---

[2] *Sit now at the feast, and disclose thy purposes to the victorious heroes, as thy spirit urges.*—Kl. reaches the above translation by erasing the comma after 'meoto' and reading 'sige-hrèðsecgum.'—There are other and bolder emendations and suggestions. Of these the boldest is to regard 'meoto' as a verb (imperative), and read 'on sæl': *Think upon gayety, etc.*—All the renderings are unsatisfactory, the one given in our translation involving a zeugma.

Thy victor-fame show, as thy spirit doth urge thee!'
> A bench is made ready for Beowulf and his party.

For the men of the Geats then together assembled,   35
In the beer-hall blithesome a bench was made ready;
There warlike in spirit they went to be seated,
Proud and exultant. A liegeman did service,
Who a beaker embellished bore with decorum,
> The gleeman sings

And gleaming-drink poured. The gleeman sang whilom 40
> The heroes all rejoice together.

Hearty in Heorot; there was heroes' rejoicing,
A numerous war-band of Weders and Danemen.

IX.

Unferth Taunts Beowulf

> Unferth, a thane of Hrothgar, is jealous of Beowulf, and
> undertakes to twit him.

Unferth spoke up, Ecglaf his son,
Who sat at the feet of the lord of the Scyldings,
Opened the jousting (the journey[1] of Beowulf,
Sea-farer doughty, gave sorrow to Unferth
And greatest chagrin, too, for granted he never   5
That any man else on earth should attain to,
Gain under heaven, more glory than he):

> Did you take part in a swimming-match with Breca?

'Art thou that Beowulf with Breca did struggle,
On the wide sea-currents at swimming contended,
Where to humor your pride the ocean ye tried,   10

> 'Twas mere folly that actuated you both to risk your lives
> on the ocean.

From vainest vaunting adventured your bodies
In care of the waters? And no one was able
Nor lief nor loth one, in the least to dissuade you

---

[1] It has been plausibly suggested that 'síð' (in 501 and in 353) means
'arrival.' If so, translate the bracket: *(the arrival of Beowulf, the brave
sea-farer, was a source of great chagrin to Unferth, etc.).*

Your difficult voyage; then ye ventured a-swimming,
Where your arms outstretching the streams
    ye did cover,   15
The mere-ways measured, mixing and stirring them,
Glided the ocean; angry the waves were,
With the weltering of winter. In the water's possession,
Ye toiled for a seven-night; he at swimming outdid thee,
In strength excelled thee. Then early at morning   20
On the Heathoremes' shore the holm-currents
    tossed him,
Sought he thenceward the home of his fathers,
Beloved of his liegemen, the land of the Brondings,
The peace-castle pleasant, where a people he wielded,
Had borough and jewels. The pledge that he made thee 25
    Breca outdid you entirely.
The son of Beanstan hath soothly accomplished.
Then I ween thou wilt find thee less fortunate issue,
    Much more will Grendel outdo you, if you vie with him in
    prowess.
Though ever triumphant in onset of battle,
A grim grappling, if Grendel thou darest
For the space of a night near-by to wait for!'   30
    Beowulf retaliates.
Beowulf answered, offspring of Ecgtheow:
'My good friend Unferth, sure freely and wildly,
    O friend Unferth, you are fuddled with beer, and cannot
    talk coherently.
Thou fuddled with beer of Breca hast spoken,
Hast told of his journey! A fact I allege it,
That greater strength in the waters I had then,   35
Ills in the ocean, than any man else had.
We made agreement as the merest of striplings
Promised each other (both of us then were
    We simply kept an engagement made in early life.
Younkers in years) that we yet would adventure

Out on the ocean; it all we accomplished. 40
While swimming the sea-floods, sword-blade
    unscabbarded
Boldly we brandished, our bodies expected
To shield from the sharks. He sure was unable
    He *could* not excel me, and I *would* not excel him.
To swim on the waters further than I could,
More swift on the waves, nor *would* I from him go. 45
Then we two companions stayed in the ocean
    After five days the currents separated us.
Five nights together, till the currents did part us,
The weltering waters, weathers the bleakest,
And nethermost night, and the north-wind whistled
Fierce in our faces; fell were the billows. 50
The mere fishes' mood was mightily ruffled:
And there against foemen my firm-knotted corslet,
Hand-jointed, hardy, help did afford me;
My battle-sark braided, brilliantly gilded,
    A horrible sea-beast attacked me, but I slew him.
Lay on my bosom. To the bottom then dragged me, 55
A hateful fiend-scather, seized me and held me,
Grim in his grapple: 'twas granted me, nathless,
To pierce the monster with the point of my weapon,
My obedient blade; battle offcarried
The mighty mere-creature by means of my hand-blow. 60

X.

Beowulf Silences Unferth—Glee is High

'So ill-meaning enemies often did cause me
Sorrow the sorest. I served them, in quittance,
>My dear sword always served me faithfully.
With my dear-lovèd sword, as in sooth it was fitting;
They missed the pleasure of feasting abundantly,
Ill-doers evil, of eating my body,   5
Of surrounding the banquet deep in the ocean;
But wounded with edges early at morning
They were stretched a-high on the strand of the ocean,
>I put a stop to the outrages of the sea-monsters.
Put to sleep with the sword, that sea-going travelers
No longer thereafter were hindered from sailing   10
The foam-dashing currents. Came a light from the east,
God's beautiful beacon; the billows subsided,
That well I could see the nesses projecting,
>Fortune helps the brave earl.
The blustering crags. Weird often saveth
The undoomed hero if doughty his valor!   15
But me did it fortune[1] to fell with my weapon

---

[1] The repetition of 'hwæðere' (574 and 578) is regarded by some scholars as a defect. B. suggests 'swá Þær' for the first: *So there it befell me, etc.*

Nine of the nickers. Of night-struggle harder
'Neath dome of the heaven heard I but rarely,
Nor of wight more woful in the waves of the ocean;
Yet I 'scaped with my life the grip of the monsters, 20
  After that escape I drifted to Finland.
Weary from travel. Then the waters bare me
To the land of the Finns, the flood with the current,
  I have never heard of your doing any such bold deeds.
The weltering waves. Not a word hath been told me
Of deeds so daring done by thee, Unferth,
And of sword-terror none; never hath Breca 25
At the play of the battle, nor either of you two,
Feat so fearless performèd with weapons
Glinting and gleaming . . . .
. . . . I utter no boasting;
  You are a slayer of brothers, and will suffer damnation, wise
  as you may be.
Though with cold-blooded cruelty thou killedst thy
  brothers, 30
Thy nearest of kin; thou needs must in hell get
Direful damnation, though doughty thy wisdom.
I tell thee in earnest, offspring of Ecglaf,
Never had Grendel such numberless horrors,
The direful demon, done to thy liegelord, 35
Harrying in Heorot, if thy heart were as sturdy,
  Had your acts been as brave as your words, Grendel had
  not ravaged your land so long.
Thy mood as ferocious as thou dost describe them.
He hath found out fully that the fierce-burning hatred,
The edge-battle eager, of all of your kindred,
Of the Victory-Scyldings, need little dismay him: 40
Oaths he exacteth, not any he spares

Another suggestion is to change the second 'hwæðere' into 'swá Þær': *So there I escaped with my life, etc.*

The monster is not afraid of the Danes,
Of the folk of the Danemen, but fighteth with pleasure,
Killeth and feasteth, no contest expecteth
    but he will soon learn to dread the Geats.
From Spear-Danish people. But the prowess and valor
Of the earls of the Geatmen early shall venture   45
To give him a grapple. He shall go who is able
Bravely to banquet, when the bright-light of morning
    On the second day, any warrior may go unmolested to the
    mead-banquet.
Which the second day bringeth, the sun in its
    ether-robes,
O'er children of men shines from the southward!'
Then the gray-haired, war-famed giver of treasure   50
    Hrothgar's spirits are revived.
Was blithesome and joyous, the Bright-Danish ruler
Expected assistance; the people's protector
    The old king trusts Beowulf. The heroes are joyful.
Heard from Beowulf his bold resolution.
There was laughter of heroes; loud was the clatter,
The words were winsome. Wealhtheow advanced then, 55
    Queen Wealhtheow plays the hostess.
Consort of Hrothgar, of courtesy mindful,
Gold-decked saluted the men in the building,
And the freeborn woman the beaker presented
    She offers the cup to her husband first.
To the lord of the kingdom, first of the East-Danes,
Bade him be blithesome when beer was a-flowing,   60
Lief to his liegemen; he lustily tasted
Of banquet and beaker, battle-famed ruler.
The Helmingish lady then graciously circled
'Mid all the liegemen lesser and greater:
    She gives presents to the heroes.
Treasure-cups tendered, till time was afforded   65
That the decorous-mooded, diademed folk-queen

Then she offers the cup to Beowulf, thanking God that aid
has come.

Might bear to Beowulf the bumper o'errunning;
She greeted the Geat-prince, God she did thank,
Most wise in her words, that her wish was accomplished,
That in any of earlmen she ever should look for   70
Solace in sorrow. He accepted the beaker,
Battle-bold warrior, at Wealhtheow's giving,

Beowulf states to the queen the object of his visit.

Then equipped for combat quoth he in measures,
Beowulf spake, offspring of Ecgtheow:
'I purposed in spirit when I mounted the ocean,   75

I determined to do or die.

When I boarded my boat with a band of my liegemen,
I would work to the fullest the will of your people
Or in foe's-clutches fastened fall in the battle.
Deeds I shall do of daring and prowess,
Or the last of my life-days live in this mead-hall.'   80
These words to the lady were welcome and pleasing,
The boast of the Geatman; with gold trappings broidered
Went the freeborn folk-queen her fond-lord to sit by.

Glee is high.

Then again as of yore was heard in the building
Courtly discussion, conquerors' shouting,   85
Heroes were happy, till Healfdene's son would
Go to his slumber to seek for refreshing;
For the horrid hell-monster in the hall-building knew he
A fight was determined,[2] since the light of the sun they
No longer could see, and lowering darkness   90
O'er all had descended, and dark under heaven
Shadowy shapes came shying around them.

[2] Kl. suggests a period after 'determined.' This would give the passage as
follows: *Since they no longer could see the light of the sun, and lowering
darkness was down over all, dire under the heavens shadowy beings came
going around them.*

Hrothgar retires, leaving Beowulf in charge of the hall.

The liegemen all rose then. One saluted the other,
Hrothgar Beowulf, in rhythmical measures,
Wishing him well, and, the wassail-hall giving   95
To his care and keeping, quoth he departing:
'Not to any one else have I ever entrusted,
But thee and thee only, the hall of the Danemen,
Since high I could heave my hand and my buckler.
Take thou in charge now the noblest of houses;   100
Be mindful of honor, exhibiting prowess,
Watch 'gainst the foeman! Thou shalt want no enjoyments,
Survive thou safely adventure so glorious!'

XI.

All Sleep save One

Hrothgar retires.

Then Hrothgar departed, his earl-throng attending him,
Folk-lord of Scyldings, forth from the building;
The war-chieftain wished then Wealhtheow to look for,
The queen for a bedmate. To keep away Grendel

God has provided a watch for the hall.

The Glory of Kings had given a hall-watch,   5
As men heard recounted: for the king of the Danemen
He did special service, gave the giant a watcher:
And the prince of the Geatmen implicitly trusted

Beowulf is self-confident.

His warlike strength and the Wielder's protection.

He prepares for rest.

His armor of iron off him he did then,   10
His helmet from his head, to his henchman committed
His chased-handled chain-sword, choicest of weapons,
And bade him bide with his battle-equipments.
The good one then uttered words of defiance,
Beowulf Geatman, ere his bed he upmounted: 15

Beowulf boasts of his ability to cope with Grendel.

'I hold me no meaner in matters of prowess,
In warlike achievements, than Grendel does himself;

Hence I seek not with sword-edge to sooth him
    to slumber,
Of life to bereave him, though well I am able.
> We will fight with nature's weapons only.

No battle-skill[1] has he, that blows he should strike me,   20
To shatter my shield, though sure he is mighty
In strife and destruction; but struggling by night we
Shall do without edges, dare he to look for
Weaponless warfare, and wise-mooded Father
The glory apportion, God ever-holy,   25
> God may decide who shall conquer

On which hand soever to him seemeth proper.'
Then the brave-mooded hero bent to his slumber,
The pillow received the cheek of the noble;
> The Geatish warriors lie down.

And many a martial mere-thane attending
Sank to his slumber. Seemed it unlikely   30
> They thought it very unlikely that they should ever see their
> homes again.

That ever thereafter any should hope to
Be happy at home, hero-friends visit
Or the lordly troop-castle where he lived from his
    childhood;
They had heard how slaughter had snatched
    from the wine-hall,
Had recently ravished, of the race of the Scyldings   35
> But God raised up a deliverer.

Too many by far. But the Lord to them granted
The weaving of war-speed, to Wederish heroes
Aid and comfort, that every opponent
By one man's war-might they worsted and vanquished,

---

[1] Gr. understood 'gódra' as meaning 'advantages in battle.' This rendering
H.-So. rejects. The latter takes the passage as meaning that Grendel, though
mighty and formidable, has no skill in the art of war.

God rules the world.

By the might of himself; the truth is established   40
That God Almighty hath governed for ages
Kindreds and nations. A night very lurid

Grendel comes to Heorot.

The trav'ler-at-twilight came tramping and striding.
The warriors were sleeping who should watch the horned-
    building,

Only one warrior is awake.

One only excepted. 'Mid earthmen 'twas 'stablished,   45
Th' implacable foeman was powerless to hurl them
To the land of shadows, if the Lord were unwilling;
But serving as warder, in terror to foemen,
He angrily bided the issue of battle.[2]

---

[2] B. in his masterly articles on *Beowulf* (P. and B. XII.) rejects the division usually made at this point, 'Þá.' (711), usually rendered 'then,' he translates 'when,' and connects its clause with the foregoing sentence. These changes he makes to reduce the number of 'cóm's' as principal verbs. (Cf. 703, 711, 721.) With all deference to this acute scholar, I must say that it seems to me that the poet is exhausting his resources to bring out clearly the supreme event on which the whole subsequent action turns. First, he (Grendel) came *in the wan night*; second, he came *from the moor*; third, he came *to the hall*. Time, place from which, place to which, are all given.

XII.

Grendel and Beowulf

Grendel comes from the fens.

'Neath the cloudy cliffs came from the moor then
Grendel going, God's anger bare he.
The monster intended some one of earthmen
In the hall-building grand to entrap and make way with:

He goes towards the joyous building.

He went under welkin where well he knew of   5
The wine-joyous building, brilliant with plating,
Gold-hall of earthmen. Not the earliest occasion

This was not his first visit there.

He the home and manor of Hrothgar had sought:
Ne'er found he in life-days later nor earlier
Hardier hero, hall-thanes[1] more sturdy!   10
Then came to the building the warrior marching,

His horrid fingers tear the door open.

Bereft of his joyance. The door quickly opened
On fire-hinges fastened, when his fingers had touched it;
The fell one had flung then—his fury so bitter—

[1] B. and t.B. emend so as to make lines 9 and 10 read: *Never in his life,
earlier or later, had he, the hell-thane, found a braver hero.*—They argue that
Beowulf's companions had done nothing to merit such encomiums as the
usual readings allow them.

Open the entrance. Early thereafter   15
The foeman trod the shining hall-pavement,

> He strides furiously into the hall.

Strode he angrily; from the eyes of him glimmered
A lustre unlovely likest to fire.
He beheld in the hall the heroes in numbers,
A circle of kinsmen sleeping together,   20

> He exults over his supposed prey.

A throng of thanemen: then his thoughts were exultant,
He minded to sunder from each of the thanemen
The life from his body, horrible demon,
Ere morning came, since fate had allowed him

> Fate has decreed that he shall devour no more heroes.
> Beowulf suffers from suspense.

The prospect of plenty. Providence willed not   25
To permit him any more of men under heaven
To eat in the night-time. Higelac's kinsman
Great sorrow endured how the dire-mooded creature
In unlooked-for assaults were likely to bear him.
No thought had the monster of deferring the matter,   30

> Grendel immediately seizes a sleeping warrior, and devours
> him.

But on earliest occasion he quickly laid hold of
A soldier asleep, suddenly tore him,
Bit his bone-prison, the blood drank in currents,
Swallowed in mouthfuls: he soon had the dead man's
Feet and hands, too, eaten entirely.   35
Nearer he strode then, the stout-hearted warrior

> Beowulf and Grendel grapple.

Snatched as he slumbered, seizing with hand-grip,
Forward the foeman foined with his hand;
Caught he quickly the cunning deviser,
On his elbow he rested. This early discovered   40
The master of malice, that in middle-earth's regions,
'Neath the whole of the heavens, no hand-grapple greater

The monster is amazed at Beowulf's strength.

In any man else had he ever encountered:
Fearful in spirit, faint-mooded waxed he,
Not off could betake him; death he was pondering,   45

He is anxious to flee.

Would fly to his covert, seek the devils' assembly:
His calling no more was the same he had followed
Long in his lifetime. The liege-kinsman worthy

Beowulf recalls his boast of the evening, and determines to
fulfil it.

Of Higelac minded his speech of the evening,
Stood he up straight and stoutly did seize him.   50
His fingers crackled; the giant was outward,
The earl stepped farther. The famous one minded
To flee away farther, if he found an occasion,
And off and away, avoiding delay,
To fly to the fen-moors; he fully was ware of   55
The strength of his grapple in the grip of the foeman.

'Twas a luckless day for Grendel.

'Twas an ill-taken journey that the injury-bringing,
Harrying harmer to Heorot wandered:

The hall groans.

The palace re-echoed; to all of the Danemen,
Dwellers in castles, to each of the bold ones,   60
Earlmen, was terror. Angry they both were,
Archwarders raging.[2] Rattled the building;
'Twas a marvellous wonder that the wine-hall withstood then
The bold-in-battle, bent not to earthward,
Excellent earth-hall; but within and without it   65
Was fastened so firmly in fetters of iron,
By the art of the armorer. Off from the sill there
Bent mead-benches many, as men have informed me,

[2] For 'réðe rén-weardas' (771), t.B. suggests 'réðe, rénhearde.' Translate:
They were both angry, raging and mighty.

Adorned with gold-work, where the grim ones did struggle.
The Scylding wise men weened ne'er before   70
That by might and main-strength a man under heaven
Might break it in pieces, bone-decked, resplendent,
Crush it by cunning, unless clutch of the fire
In smoke should consume it. The sound mounted upward

> Grendel's cries terrify the Danes.

Novel enough; on the North Danes fastened   75
A terror of anguish, on all of the men there
Who heard from the wall the weeping and plaining,
The song of defeat from the foeman of heaven,
Heard him hymns of horror howl, and his sorrow
Hell-bound bewailing. He held him too firmly   80
Who was strongest of main-strength of men of that era.

XIII.

Grendel is Vanquished

Beowulf has no idea of letting Grendel live.
For no cause whatever would the earlmen's defender
Leave in life-joys the loathsome newcomer,
He deemed his existence utterly useless
To men under heaven. Many a noble
Of Beowulf brandished his battle-sword old,   5
Would guard the life of his lord and protector,
The far-famed chieftain, if able to do so;
While waging the warfare, this wist they but little,
Brave battle-thanes, while his body intending
No weapon would harm Grendel; he bore a charmed life.
To slit into slivers, and seeking his spirit: 10
That the relentless foeman nor finest of weapons
Of all on the earth, nor any of war-bills
Was willing to injure; but weapons of victory
Swords and suchlike he had sworn to dispense with.
His death at that time must prove to be wretched,   15
And the far-away spirit widely should journey
Into enemies' power. This plainly he saw then
Who with mirth[1] of mood malice no little

---

[1] It has been proposed to translate 'myrðe' by *with sorrow*; but there seems

Had wrought in the past on the race of the earthmen
(To God he was hostile), that his body would fail him,   20
But Higelac's hardy henchman and kinsman
Held him by the hand; hateful to other

> Grendel is sorely wounded.

Was each one if living. A body-wound suffered
The direful demon, damage incurable

> His body bursts.

Was seen on his shoulder, his sinews were shivered,   25
His body did burst. To Beowulf was given
Glory in battle; Grendel from thenceward
Must flee and hide him in the fen-cliffs and marshes,
Sick unto death, his dwelling must look for
Unwinsome and woful; he wist the more fully   30

> The monster flees away to hide in the moors.

The end of his earthly existence was nearing,
His life-days' limits. At last for the Danemen,
When the slaughter was over, their wish was accomplished.
The comer-from-far-land had cleansed then of evil,
Wise and valiant, the war-hall of Hrothgar,   35
Saved it from violence. He joyed in the night-work,
In repute for prowess; the prince of the Geatmen
For the East-Danish people his boast had accomplished,
Bettered their burdensome bale-sorrows fully,
The craft-begot evil they erstwhile had suffered   40
And were forced to endure from crushing oppression,
Their manifold misery. 'Twas a manifest token,

> Beowulf suspends Grendel's hand and arm in Heorot.

When the hero-in-battle the hand suspended,
The arm and the shoulder (there was all of the claw
Of Grendel together) 'neath great-stretching hall-roof.   45

---

no authority for such a rendering. To the present translator, the phrase
'módes myrðe' seems a mere padding for *gladly*; i.e., *he who gladly harassed
mankind*.

XIV.

Rejoicing of the Danes

At early dawn, warriors from far and near come together to
hear of the night's adventures.

In the mist of the morning many a warrior
Stood round the gift-hall, as the story is told me:
Folk-princes fared then from far and from near
Through long-stretching journeys to look at the wonder,
The footprints of the foeman. Few of the warriors   5

Few warriors lamented Grendel's destruction.

Who gazed on the foot-tracks of the inglorious creature
His parting from life pained very deeply,
How, weary in spirit, off from those regions
In combats conquered he carried his traces,
Fated and flying, to the flood of the nickers.   10

Grendel's blood dyes the waters.

There in bloody billows bubbled the currents,
The angry eddy was everywhere mingled
And seething with gore, welling with sword-blood;[1]
He death-doomed had hid him, when reaved of his joyance

---

[1] S. emends, suggesting 'déop' for 'déog,' and removing semicolon after 'wéol.'
The two half-lines 'welling . . . hid him' would then read: *The bloody deep
welled with sword-gore*. B. accepts 'déop' for 'déog,' but reads 'déaŏ-fæges':
The deep boiled with the sword-gore of the death-doomed one.

He laid down his life in the lair he had fled to,   15
His heathenish spirit, where hell did receive him.
Thence the friends from of old backward turned them,
And many a younker from merry adventure,
Striding their stallions, stout from the seaward,
Heroes on horses. There were heard very often   20

> Beowulf is the hero of the hour.

Beowulf's praises; many often asserted
That neither south nor north, in the circuit of waters,

> He is regarded as a probable successor to Hrothgar.

O'er outstretching earth-plain, none other was better
'Mid bearers of war-shields, more worthy to govern,
'Neath the arch of the ether. Not any, however,   25
'Gainst the friend-lord muttered, mocking-words uttered

> But no word is uttered to derogate from the old king

Of Hrothgar the gracious (a good king he).
Oft the famed ones permitted their fallow-skinned horses
To run in rivalry, racing and chasing,
Where the fieldways appeared to them fair and inviting, 30
Known for their excellence; oft a thane of the folk-lord,[2]

> The gleeman sings the deeds of heroes.

[3]A man of celebrity, mindful of rhythms,
Who ancient traditions treasured in memory,
New word-groups found properly bound:
The bard after 'gan then Beowulf's venture   35

> He sings in alliterative measures of Beowulf's prowess.

Wisely to tell of, and words that were clever
To utter skilfully, earnestly speaking,

---

[2] Another and quite different rendering of this passage is as follows: *Oft a liegeman of the king, a fame-covered man mindful of songs, who very many ancient traditions remembered (he found other word-groups accurately bound together) began afterward to tell of Beowulf's adventure, skilfully to narrate it, etc.*

[3] Might 'guma gilp-hladen' mean 'a man laden with boasts of the deeds of others'?

Everything told he that he heard as to Sigmund's

Also of Sigemund, who has slain a great fire-dragon.

Mighty achievements, many things hidden,
The strife of the Wælsing, the wide-going ventures   40
The children of men knew of but little,
The feud and the fury, but Fitela with him,
When suchlike matters he minded to speak of,
Uncle to nephew, as in every contention
Each to other was ever devoted: 45
A numerous host of the race of the scathers
They had slain with the sword-edge. To Sigmund accrued then
No little of glory, when his life-days were over,
Since he sturdy in struggle had destroyed the great dragon,
The hoard-treasure's keeper; 'neath the hoar-grayish
    stone he,   50
The son of the atheling, unaided adventured
The perilous project; not present was Fitela,
Yet the fortune befell him of forcing his weapon
Through the marvellous dragon, that it stood in the wall,
Well-honored weapon; the worm was slaughtered.   55
The great one had gained then by his glorious achievement
To reap from the ring-hoard richest enjoyment,
As best it did please him: his vessel he loaded,
Shining ornaments on the ship's bosom carried,
Kinsman of Wæls: the drake in heat melted.   60

Sigemund was widely famed.

He was farthest famed of fugitive pilgrims,
Mid wide-scattered world-folk, for works of great prowess,
War-troopers' shelter: hence waxed he in honor.[4]

Heremod, an unfortunate Danish king, is introduced by way
of contrast.

---

[4] t.B. accepts B.'s 'hé þæs áron þáh' as given by H.-So., but puts a comma
after 'þáh,' and takes 'siððan' as introducing a dependent clause: *He throve
in honor since Heremod's strength . . . had decreased.*

Afterward Heremod's hero-strength failed him,
His vigor and valor. 'Mid venomous haters   65
To the hands of foemen he was foully delivered,
Offdriven early. Agony-billows

> Unlike Sigemund and Beowulf, Heremod was a burden to
> his people.

Oppressed him too long, to his people he became then,
To all the athelings, an ever-great burden;
And the daring one's journey in days of yore   70
Many wise men were wont to deplore,
Such as hoped he would bring them help in their sorrow,
That the son of their ruler should rise into power,
Holding the headship held by his fathers,
Should govern the people, the gold-hoard and borough,   75
The kingdom of heroes, the realm of the Scyldings.

> Beowulf is an honor to his race.

He to all men became then far more beloved,
Higelac's kinsman, to kindreds and races,
To his friends much dearer; him malice assaulted.—

> The story is resumed.

Oft running and racing on roadsters they measured   80
The dun-colored highways. Then the light of the morning
Was hurried and hastened. Went henchmen in numbers
To the beautiful building, bold ones in spirit,
To look at the wonder; the liegelord himself then
From his wife-bower wending, warden of treasures,   85
Glorious trod with troopers unnumbered,
Famed for his virtues, and with him the queen-wife
Measured the mead-ways, with maidens attending.

XV.

Hrothgar's Gratitude

Hrothgar discoursed (to the hall-building went he,
He stood by the pillar,[1] saw the steep-rising hall-roof
Gleaming with gold-gems, and Grendel his hand there):

> Hrothgar gives thanks for the overthrow of the monster.

'For the sight we behold now, thanks to the Wielder
Early be offered! Much evil I bided,   5
Snaring from Grendel:[2] God can e'er 'complish
Wonder on wonder, Wielder of Glory!

> I had given up all hope, when this brave liegeman came to
> our aid.

But lately I reckoned ne'er under heaven
Comfort to gain me for any of sorrows,
While the handsomest of houses horrid with bloodstain   10
Gory uptowered; grief had off-frightened[3]
Each of the wise ones who weened not that ever

---

[1] B. and t.B. read 'staþole,' and translate *stood on the floor*.
[2] For 'snaring from Grendel,' 'sorrows at Grendel's hands' has been
suggested. This gives a parallel to 'láðes.' 'Grynna' may well be gen. pl. of
'gyrn,' by a scribal slip.
[3] The H.-So punctuation has been followed; but B. has been followed in
understanding 'gehwylcne' as object of 'wíd-scofen (hæfde).' Gr. construes
'wéa' as nom abs.

The folk-troop's defences 'gainst foes they should strengthen,
'Gainst sprites and monsters. Through the might of the Wielder
A doughty retainer hath a deed now accomplished   15
Which erstwhile we all with our excellent wisdom

> If his mother yet liveth, well may she thank God for this son.

Failed to perform. May affirm very truly
What woman soever in all of the nations
Gave birth to the child, if yet she surviveth,
That the long-ruling Lord was lavish to herward   20
In the birth of the bairn. Now, Beowulf dear,

> Hereafter, Beowulf, thou shalt be my son.

Most excellent hero, I'll love thee in spirit
As bairn of my body; bear well henceforward
The relationship new. No lack shall befall thee
Of earth-joys any I ever can give thee.   25
Full often for lesser service I've given
Hero less hardy hoard-treasure precious,

> Thou hast won immortal distinction.

To a weaker in war-strife. By works of distinction
Thou hast gained for thyself now that thy glory shall flourish
Forever and ever. The All-Ruler quite thee   30
With good from His hand as He hitherto did thee!'

> Beowulf replies: I was most happy to render thee this service.

Beowulf answered, Ecgtheow's offspring:
'That labor of glory most gladly achieved we,
The combat accomplished, unquailing we ventured
The enemy's grapple; I would grant it much rather   35
Thou wert able to look at the creature in person,
Faint unto falling, the foe in his trappings!
On murder-bed quickly I minded to bind him,
With firm-holding fetters, that forced by my grapple
Low he should lie in life-and-death struggle   40
'Less his body escape; I was wholly unable,

> I could not keep the monster from escaping, as God did not
> will that I should.

Since God did not will it, to keep him from going,
Not held him that firmly, hated opposer;
Too swift was the foeman. Yet safety regarding
He suffered his hand behind him to linger,   45
His arm and shoulder, to act as watcher;
>   He left his hand and arm behind.
No shadow of solace the woe-begone creature
Found him there nathless: the hated destroyer
Liveth no longer, lashed for his evils,
But sorrow hath seized him, in snare-meshes hath him   50
Close in its clutches, keepeth him writhing
In baleful bonds: there banished for evil
The man shall wait for the mighty tribunal,
>   God will give him his deserts.
How the God of glory shall give him his earnings.'
Then the soldier kept silent, son of old Ecglaf,   55
>   Unferth has nothing more to say, for Beowulf's actions speak
>   louder than words.
From boasting and bragging of battle-achievements,
Since the princes beheld there the hand that depended
'Neath the lofty hall-timbers by the might of the nobleman,
Each one before him, the enemy's fingers;
Each finger-nail strong steel most resembled,   60
The heathen one's hand-spur, the hero-in-battle's
Claw most uncanny; quoth they agreeing,
>   No sword will harm the monster.
That not any excellent edges of brave ones
Was willing to touch him, the terrible creature's
Battle-hand bloody to bear away from him.   65

XVI.

Hrothgar Lavishes Gifts upon his Deliverer

Heorot is adorned with hands.

Then straight was ordered that Heorot inside[1]
With hands be embellished: a host of them gathered,
Of men and women, who the wassailing-building
The guest-hall begeared. Gold-flashing sparkled
Webs on the walls then, of wonders a many   5
To each of the heroes that look on such objects.

The hall is defaced, however.

The beautiful building was broken to pieces
Which all within with irons was fastened,
Its hinges torn off: only the roof was
Whole and uninjured when the horrible creature   10
Outlawed for evil off had betaken him,
Hopeless of living. 'Tis hard to avoid it

[A vague passage of five verses.]

---

[1] Kl. suggests 'hroden' for 'háten,' and renders: *Then quickly was Heorot adorned within, with hands bedecked.*—B. suggests 'gefrætwon' instead of 'gefrætwod,' and renders: *Then was it commanded to adorn Heorot within quickly with hands.*—The former has the advantage of affording a parallel to 'gefrætwod': both have the disadvantage of altering the text.

(Whoever will do it!); but he doubtless must come to[2]
The place awaiting, as Wyrd hath appointed,
Soul-bearers, earth-dwellers, earls under heaven,   15
Where bound on its bed his body shall slumber

> Hrothgar goes to the banquet.

When feasting is finished. Full was the time then
That the son of Healfdene went to the building;
The excellent atheling would eat of the banquet.
Ne'er heard I that people with hero-band larger   20
Bare them better tow'rds their bracelet-bestower.
The laden-with-glory stooped to the bench then
(Their kinsmen-companions in plenty were joyful,
Many a cupful quaffing complaisantly),
Doughty of spirit in the high-tow'ring palace,   25

> Hrothgar's nephew, Hrothulf, is present.

Hrothgar and Hrothulf. Heorot then inside
Was filled with friendly ones; falsehood and treachery
The Folk-Scyldings now nowise did practise.

> Hrothgar lavishes gifts upon Beowulf.

Then the offspring of Healfdene offered to Beowulf
A golden standard, as reward for the victory,   30
A banner embossed, burnie and helmet;
Many men saw then a song-famous weapon
Borne 'fore the hero. Beowulf drank of
The cup in the building; that treasure-bestowing
He needed not blush for in battle-men's presence.   35

> Four handsomer gifts were never presented.

Ne'er heard I that many men on the ale-bench
In friendlier fashion to their fellows presented

---

[2] The passage 1005—1009 seems to be hopeless. One difficult point is to
find a subject for 'gesacan.' Some say 'he'; others supply 'each,' *i.e., every
soul-bearer . . . must gain the inevitable place.* The genitives in this case
are partitive.—If 'he' be subj., the genitives are dependent on 'gearwe' (=
prepared).—The 'he' itself is disputed, some referring it to Grendel; but B.
takes it as involved in the parenthesis.

Four bright jewels with gold-work embellished.
'Round the roof of the helmet a head-guarder outside
Braided with wires, with bosses was furnished,   40
That swords-for-the-battle fight-hardened might fail
Boldly to harm him, when the hero proceeded

> Hrothgar commands that eight finely caparisoned steeds be
> brought to Beowulf.

Forth against foemen. The defender of earls then
Commanded that eight steeds with bridles
Gold-plated, gleaming, be guided to hallward,   45
Inside the building; on one of them stood then
An art-broidered saddle embellished with jewels;
'Twas the sovereign's seat, when the son of King Healfdene
Was pleased to take part in the play of the edges;
The famous one's valor ne'er failed at the front when   50
Slain ones were bowing. And to Beowulf granted
The prince of the Ingwins, power over both,
O'er war-steeds and weapons; bade him well to enjoy them.
In so manly a manner the mighty-famed chieftain,
Hoard-ward of heroes, with horses and jewels   55
War-storms requited, that none e'er condemneth
Who willeth to tell truth with full justice.

XVII.

Banquet (*Continued*)—The Scop's Song of Finn and Hnæf

Each of Beowulf's companions receives a costly gift.

And the atheling of earlmen to each of the heroes
Who the ways of the waters went with Beowulf,
A costly gift-token gave on the mead-bench,
Offered an heirloom, and ordered that that man

The warrior killed by Grendel is to be paid for in gold.

With gold should be paid for, whom Grendel
    had erstwhile   5
Wickedly slaughtered, as he more of them had done
Had far-seeing God and the mood of the hero
The fate not averted: the Father then governed
All of the earth-dwellers, as He ever is doing;
Hence insight for all men is everywhere fittest,   10
Forethought of spirit! much he shall suffer
Of lief and of loathsome who long in this present
Useth the world in this woful existence.
There was music and merriment mingling together

Hrothgar's scop recalls events in the reign of his lord's father.

Touching Healfdene's leader; the joy-wood was
    fingered,   15
Measures recited, when the singer of Hrothgar

On mead-bench should mention the merry hall-joyance
Of the kinsmen of Finn, when onset surprised them:

> Hnæf, the Danish general, is treacherously attacked while
> staying at Finn's castle.

'The Half-Danish hero, Hnæf of the Scyldings,
On the field of the Frisians was fated to perish.　　　　20
Sure Hildeburg needed not mention approving
The faith of the Jutemen: though blámeless entirely,

> Queen Hildeburg is not only wife of Finn, but a kinswoman
> of the murdered Hnæf.

When shields were shivered she was shorn of her darlings,
Of bairns and brothers: they bent to their fate
With war-spear wounded; woe was that woman.　　　　25
Not causeless lamented the daughter of Hoce
The decree of the Wielder when morning-light came and
She was able 'neath heaven to behold the destruction
Of brothers and bairns, where the brightest of earth-joys

> Finn's force is almost exterminated.

She had hitherto had: all the henchmen of Finn　　　　30
War had offtaken, save a handful remaining,
That he nowise was able to offer resistance[1]

> Hengest succeeds Hnæf as Danish general.

To the onset of Hengest in the parley of battle,
Nor the wretched remnant to rescue in war from
The earl of the atheling; but they offered conditions,　　　　35

> Compact between the Frisians and the Danes.

Another great building to fully make ready,
A hall and a high-seat, that half they might rule with
The sons of the Jutemen, and that Folcwalda's son would
Day after day the Danemen honor
When gifts were giving, and grant of his ring-store　　　　40

---

[1] For 1084, R. suggests 'wiht Hengeste wið gefeohtan.'—K. suggests 'wið
Hengeste wiht gefeohtan.' Neither emendation would make any essential
change in the translation.

To Hengest's earl-troop ever so freely,
Of his gold-plated jewels, as he encouraged the Frisians
  Equality of gifts agreed on.
On the bench of the beer-hall. On both sides they swore then
A fast-binding compact; Finn unto Hengest
With no thought of revoking vowed then most solemnly 45
The woe-begone remnant well to take charge of,
His Witan advising; the agreement should no one
By words or works weaken and shatter,
By artifice ever injure its value,
Though reaved of their ruler their ring-giver's slayer 50
They followed as vassals, Fate so requiring:
  No one shall refer to old grudges.
Then if one of the Frisians the quarrel should speak of
In tones that were taunting, terrible edges
Should cut in requital. Accomplished the oath was,
And treasure of gold from the hoard was uplifted. 55
  Danish warriors are burned on a funeral-pyre.
The best of the Scylding braves was then fully
Prepared for the pile; at the pyre was seen clearly
The blood-gory burnie, the boar with his gilding,
The iron-hard swine, athelings many
Fatally wounded; no few had been slaughtered. 60
Hildeburg bade then, at the burning of Hnæf,
  Queen Hildeburg has her son burnt along with Hnæf.
The bairn of her bosom to bear to the fire,
That his body be burned and borne to the pyre.
The woe-stricken woman wept on his shoulder,[2]

---

[2] The separation of adjective and noun by a phrase (cf. v. 1118) being very unusual, some scholars have put 'earme on eaxle' with the foregoing lines, inserting a semicolon after 'eaxle.' In this case 'on eaxe' (*i.e.*, on the ashes, cinders) is sometimes read, and this affords a parallel to 'on bæl.' Let us hope that a satisfactory rendering shall yet be reached without resorting to any tampering with the text, such as Lichtenheld proposed: 'earme ides on eaxle gnornode.'

In measures lamented; upmounted the hero.[3]   65
The greatest of dead-fires curled to the welkin,
On the hill's-front crackled; heads were a-melting,
Wound-doors bursting, while the blood was a-coursing
From body-bite fierce. The fire devoured them,
Greediest of spirits, whom war had offcarried   70
From both of the peoples; their bravest were fallen.

[3] For 'gúð-rinc,' 'gúð-réc,' *battle-smoke*, has been suggested.

XVIII.

The Finn Episode (*Continued*)—The Banquet Continues

The survivors go to Friesland, the home of Finn.

'Then the warriors departed to go to their dwellings,
Reaved of their friends, Friesland to visit,
Their homes and high-city. Hengest continued

Hengest remains there all winter, unable to get away.

Biding with Finn the blood-tainted winter,
Wholly unsundered;[1] of fatherland thought he   5
Though unable to drive the ring-stemmèd vessel
O'er the ways of the waters; the wave-deeps were tossing,
Fought with the wind; winter in ice-bonds
Closed up the currents, till there came to the dwelling
A year in its course, as yet it revolveth,   10

---

[1] For 1130 (1) R. and Gr. suggest 'elne unflitme' as 1098 (1) reads. The latter verse is undisputed; and, for the former, 'elne' would be as possible as 'ealles,' and 'unflitme' is well supported. Accepting 'elne unflitme' for both, I would suggest '*very peaceably*' for both places: (1) *Finn to Hengest very peaceably vowed with oaths*, etc. (2) *Hengest then still the slaughter-stained winter remained there with Finn very peaceably.* The two passages become thus correlatives, the second a sequel of the first. 'Elne,' in the sense of very (swíðe), needs no argument; and 'unflitme' (from 'flítan') can, it seems to me, be more plausibly rendered 'peaceful,' 'peaceable,' than 'contestable,' or 'conquerable.'

If season propitious one alway regardeth,
World-cheering weathers. Then winter was gone,
Earth's bosom was lovely; the exile would get him,

> He devises schemes of vengeance.

The guest from the palace; on grewsomest vengeance
He brooded more eager than on oversea journeys,   15
Whe'r onset-of-anger he were able to 'complish,
The bairns of the Jutemen therein to remember.
Nowise refused he the duties of liegeman
When Hun of the Frisians the battle-sword Láfing,
Fairest of falchions, friendly did give him: 20
Its edges were famous in folk-talk of Jutland.
And savage sword-fury seized in its clutches
Bold-mooded Finn where he bode in his palace,

> Guthlaf and Oslaf revenge Hnæf's slaughter.

When the grewsome grapple Guthlaf and Oslaf
Had mournfully mentioned, the mere-journey over,   25
For sorrows half-blamed him; the flickering spirit
Could not bide in his bosom. Then the building was covered[2]

> Finn is slain.

With corpses of foemen, and Finn too was slaughtered,
The king with his comrades, and the queen made a prisoner.

> The jewels of Finn, and his queen are carried away by the
> Danes.

The troops of the Scyldings bore to their vessels   30
All that the land-king had in his palace,
Such trinkets and treasures they took as, on searching,
At Finn's they could find. They ferried to Daneland
The excellent woman on oversea journey,

> The lay is concluded, and the main story is resumed.

Led her to their land-folk.' The lay was concluded,   35

---

[2] Some scholars have proposed 'roden'; the line would then read: *Then the building was reddened, etc.*, instead of 'covered.' The 'h' may have been carried over from the three alliterating 'h's.'

The gleeman's recital. Shouts again rose then,
Bench-glee resounded, bearers then offered
    Skinkers carry round the beaker.
Wine from wonder-vats. Wealhtheo advanced then
Going 'neath gold-crown, where the good ones were seated
      Queen Wealhtheow greets Hrothgar, as he sits beside
      Hrothulf, his nephew.
Uncle and nephew; their peace was yet mutual,   40
True each to the other. And Unferth the spokesman
Sat at the feet of the lord of the Scyldings:
Each trusted his spirit that his mood was courageous,
Though at fight he had failed in faith to his kinsmen.
Said the queen of the Scyldings: 'My lord and
      protector,   45
Treasure-bestower, take thou this beaker;
Joyance attend thee, gold-friend of heroes,
    Be generous to the Geats.
And greet thou the Geatmen with gracious responses!
So ought one to do. Be kind to the Geatmen,
In gifts not niggardly; anear and afar now   50
Peace thou enjoyest. Report hath informed me
Thou'lt have for a bairn the battle-brave hero.
Now is Heorot cleansèd, ring-palace gleaming;
    Have as much joy as possible in thy hall, once more purified.
Give while thou mayest many rewards,
And bequeath to thy kinsmen kingdom and people,   55
On wending thy way to the Wielder's splendor.
I know good Hrothulf, that the noble young troopers
    I know that Hrothulf will prove faithful if he survive thee.
He'll care for and honor, lord of the Scyldings,
If earth-joys thou endest earlier than he doth;
I reckon that recompense he'll render with kindness   60
Our offspring and issue, if that all he remember,
What favors of yore, when he yet was an infant,
We awarded to him for his worship and pleasure.'

Then she turned by the bench where her sons were carousing,
Hrethric and Hrothmund, and the heroes' offspring,   65

> Beowulf is sitting by the two royal sons.

The war-youth together; there the good one was sitting
'Twixt the brothers twain, Beowulf Geatman.

XIX.

Beowulf Receives Further Honor

      More gifts are offered Beowulf.
A beaker was borne him, and bidding to quaff it
Graciously given, and gold that was twisted
Pleasantly proffered, a pair of arm-jewels,
Rings and corslet, of collars the greatest
I've heard of 'neath heaven. Of heroes not any   5
More splendid from jewels have I heard 'neath the welkin,
      A famous necklace is referred to, in comparison with the
      gems presented to Beowulf.
Since Hama off bore the Brosingmen's necklace,
The bracteates and jewels, from the bright-shining city,[1]
Eormenric's cunning craftiness fled from,
Chose gain everlasting. Geatish Higelac,   10
Grandson of Swerting, last had this jewel
When tramping 'neath banner the treasure he guarded,
The field-spoil defended; Fate offcarried him
When for deeds of daring he endured tribulation,
Hate from the Frisians; the ornaments bare he   15
O'er the cup of the currents, costly gem-treasures,

---

[1] C. suggests a semicolon after 'city,' with 'he' as supplied subject of 'fled' and 'chose.'

Mighty folk-leader, he fell 'neath his target;
The[2] corpse of the king then came into charge of
The race of the Frankmen, the mail-shirt and collar:
Warmen less noble plundered the fallen,   20
When the fight was finished; the folk of the Geatmen
The field of the dead held in possession.
The choicest of mead-halls with cheering resounded.
Wealhtheow discoursed, the war-troop addressed she:

> Queen Wealhtheow magnifies Beowulf's achievements.

'This collar enjoy thou, Beowulf worthy,   25
Young man, in safety, and use thou this armor,
Gems of the people, and prosper thou fully,
Show thyself sturdy and be to these liegemen
Mild with instruction! I'll mind thy requital.
Thou hast brought it to pass that far and near   30
Forever and ever earthmen shall honor thee,
Even so widely as ocean surroundeth
The blustering bluffs. Be, while thou livest,
A wealth-blessèd atheling. I wish thee most truly

> May gifts never fail thee.

Jewels and treasure. Be kind to my son, thou   35
Living in joyance! Here each of the nobles
Is true unto other, gentle in spirit,
Loyal to leader. The liegemen are peaceful,
The war-troops ready: well-drunken heroes,[3]
Do as I bid ye.' Then she went to the settle.   40
There was choicest of banquets, wine drank the heroes:

> They little know of the sorrow in store for them.

Weird they knew not, destiny cruel,
As to many an earlman early it happened,

---

[2] For 'feorh' S. suggests 'feoh': 'corpse' in the translation would then be changed to '*possessions*,' '*belongings*.' This is a better reading than one joining, in such intimate syntactical relations, things so unlike as 'corpse' and 'jewels.'

[3] S. suggests '*wine-joyous heroes*,' '*warriors elated with wine*.'

When evening had come and Hrothgar had parted
Off to his manor, the mighty to slumber.   45
Warriors unnumbered warded the building
As erst they did often: the ale-settle bared they,
'Twas covered all over with beds and pillows.
    A doomed thane is there with them.
Doomed unto death, down to his slumber
Bowed then a beer-thane. Their battle-shields placed
   they,   50
Bright-shining targets, up by their heads then;
O'er the atheling on ale-bench 'twas easy to see there
Battle-high helmet, burnie of ring-mail,
    They were always ready for battle.
And mighty war-spear. 'Twas the wont of that people
To constantly keep them equipped for the battle,[4]   55
At home or marching—in either condition—
At seasons just such as necessity ordered
As best for their ruler; that people was worthy.

---

[4] I believe this translation brings out the meaning of the poet, without departing seriously from the H.-So. text. 'Oft' frequently means 'constantly,' 'continually,' not always 'often.'—Why 'an (on) wíg gearwe' should be written 'ánwíg-gearwe' (= ready for single combat), I cannot see. 'Gearwe' occurs quite frequently with 'on'; cf. B. 1110 (*ready for the pyre*), El. 222 (*ready for the glad journey*). Moreover, what has the idea of single combat to do with B. 1247 ff.? The poet is giving an inventory of the arms and armor which they lay aside on retiring, and he closes his narration by saying that they were *always prepared for battle both at home and on the march.*

XX.

The Mother of Grendel

They sank then to slumber. With sorrow one paid for
His evening repose, as often betid them
While Grendel was holding[1] the gold-bedecked palace,
Ill-deeds performing, till his end overtook him,
Death for his sins. 'Twas seen very clearly,   5

> Grendel's mother is known to be thirsting for revenge.

Known unto earth-folk, that still an avenger
Outlived the loathed one, long since the sorrow
Caused by the struggle; the mother of Grendel,
Devil-shaped woman, her woe ever minded,
Who was held to inhabit the horrible waters,   10

> [Grendel's progenitor, Cain, is again referred to.]

The cold-flowing currents, after Cain had become a
Slayer-with-edges to his one only brother,
The son of his sire; he set out then banished,
Marked as a murderer, man-joys avoiding,
Lived in the desert. Thence demons unnumbered   15

> The poet again magnifies Beowulf's valor.

---

[1] Several eminent authorities either read or emend the MS. so as to make this verse read, *While Grendel was wasting the gold-bedecked palace.* So 20 15 below: *ravaged the desert.*

Fate-sent awoke; one of them Grendel,
Sword-cursèd, hateful, who at Heorot met with
A man that was watching, waiting the struggle,
Where a horrid one held him with hand-grapple sturdy;
Nathless he minded the might of his body,   20
The glorious gift God had allowed him,
And folk-ruling Father's favor relied on,
His help and His comfort: so he conquered the foeman,
The hell-spirit humbled: he unhappy departed then,
Reaved of his joyance, journeying to death-haunts,   25
Foeman of man. His mother moreover

        Grendel's mother comes to avenge her son.

Eager and gloomy was anxious to go on
Her mournful mission, mindful of vengeance
For the death of her son. She came then to Heorot
Where the Armor-Dane earlmen all through the
    building   30
Were lying in slumber. Soon there became then
Return[2] to the nobles, when the mother of Grendel
Entered the folk-hall; the fear was less grievous
By even so much as the vigor of maidens,
War-strength of women, by warrior is reckoned,   35
When well-carved weapon, worked with the hammer,
Blade very bloody, brave with its edges,
Strikes down the boar-sign that stands on the helmet.
Then the hard-edgèd weapon was heaved in the building,[3]
The brand o'er the benches, broad-lindens many   40
Hand-fast were lifted; for helmet he recked not,
For armor-net broad, whom terror laid hold of.

---

[2] For 'sóna' (1281), t.B. suggests 'sára,' limiting 'edhwyrft.' Read then: *Return of sorrows to the nobles, etc.* This emendation supplies the syntactical gap after 'edhwyrft.'

[3] Some authorities follow Grein's lexicon in treating 'heard ecg' as an adj. limiting 'sweord': H.-So. renders it as a subst. (So v. 1491.) The sense of the translation would be the same.

She went then hastily, outward would get her
Her life for to save, when some one did spy her;

She seizes a favorite liegemen of Hrothgar's.

Soon she had grappled one of the athelings   45
Fast and firmly, when fenward she hied her;
That one to Hrothgar was liefest of heroes
In rank of retainer where waters encircle,
A mighty shield-warrior, whom she murdered at slumber,
A broadly-famed battle-knight. Beowulf was absent,   50

Beowulf was asleep in another part of the palace.

But another apartment was erstwhile devoted
To the glory-decked Geatman when gold was distributed.
There was hubbub in Heorot. The hand that was famous
She grasped in its gore;[4] grief was renewed then
In homes and houses: 'twas no happy arrangement   55
In both of the quarters to barter and purchase
With lives of their friends. Then the well-agèd ruler,
The gray-headed war-thane, was woful in spirit,
When his long-trusted liegeman lifeless he knew of,

Beowulf is sent for.

His dearest one gone. Quick from a room was   60
Beowulf brought, brave and triumphant.
As day was dawning in the dusk of the morning,

He comes at Hrothgar's summons.

Went then that earlman, champion noble,
Came with comrades, where the clever one bided
Whether God all gracious would grant him a respite   65
After the woe he had suffered. The war-worthy hero

---

[4] B. suggests 'under hróf genam' (v. 1303). This emendation, as well as
an emendation with (?) to v. 739, he offers, because 'under' baffles him in
both passages. All we need is to take 'under' in its secondary meaning of
'in,' which, though not given by Grein, occurs in the literature. Cf. Chron.
876 (March's A.-S. Gram. § 355) and Oro. Amaz. I. 10, where 'under' =
in the midst of. Cf. modern Eng. 'in such circumstances,' which interchanges
in good usage with 'under such circumstances.'

With a troop of retainers trod then the pavement
(The hall-building groaned), till he greeted the wise one,

Beowulf inquires how Hrothgar had enjoyed his night's rest.

The earl of the Ingwins;[5] asked if the night had
Fully refreshed him, as fain he would have it.   70

---

[5] For 'néod-laðu' (1321) C. suggests 'néad-láðum,' and translates: *asked whether the night had been pleasant to him after crushing-hostility.*

XXI.

Hrothgar's Account of the Monsters

Hrothgar laments the death of Æschere, his shoulder-
companion.

Hrothgar rejoined, helm of the Scyldings:
'Ask not of joyance! Grief is renewed to
The folk of the Danemen. Dead is Æschere,
Yrmenlaf's brother, older than he,
My true-hearted counsellor, trusty adviser,   5
Shoulder-companion, when fighting in battle
Our heads we protected, when troopers were clashing,
> He was my ideal hero.

And heroes were dashing; such an earl should be ever,
An erst-worthy atheling, as Æschere proved him.
The flickering death-spirit became in Heorot   10
His hand-to-hand murderer; I can not tell whither
The cruel one turned in the carcass exulting,
> This horrible creature came to avenge Grendel's death.

By cramming discovered.[1] The quarrel she wreaked then,
That last night igone Grendel thou killedst
In grewsomest manner, with grim-holding clutches,   15

---

[1] For 'gefrægnod' (1334), K. and t.B. suggest 'gefægnod,' rendering
'*rejoicing in her fill*.' This gives a parallel to 'æse wlanc' (1333).

Since too long he had lessened my liege-troop and wasted
My folk-men so foully. He fell in the battle
With forfeit of life, and another has followed,
A mighty crime-worker, her kinsman avenging,
And henceforth hath 'stablished her hatred unyielding,[2] 20
As it well may appear to many a liegeman,
Who mourneth in spirit the treasure-bestower,
Her heavy heart-sorrow; the hand is now lifeless
Which[3] availed you in every wish that you cherished.

> I have heard my vassals speak of these two uncanny monsters
> who lived in the moors.

Land-people heard I, liegemen, this saying,   25
Dwellers in halls, they had seen very often
A pair of such mighty march-striding creatures,
Far-dwelling spirits, holding the moorlands:
One of them wore, as well they might notice,
The image of woman, the other one wretched   30
In guise of a man wandered in exile,
Except he was huger than any of earthmen;
Earth-dwelling people entitled him Grendel
In days of yore: they know not their father,
Whe'r ill-going spirits any were borne him   35

> The inhabit the most desolate and horrible places.

Ever before. They guard the wolf-coverts,
Lands inaccessible, wind-beaten nesses,
Fearfullest fen-deeps, where a flood from the mountains
'Neath mists of the nesses netherward rattles,
The stream under earth: not far is it henceward   40
Measured by mile-lengths that the mere-water standeth,
Which forests hang over, with frost-whiting covered,[4]

---

[2] The line 'And . . . yielding,' B. renders: *And she has performed a deed of blood-vengeance whose effect is far-reaching.*

[3] 'Sé Þe' (1345) is an instance of masc. rel. with fem. antecedent. So v. 1888, where 'sé Þe' refers to 'yldo.'

[4] For 'hrímge' in the H.-So. edition, Gr. and others read 'hrínde' (=hrínende), and translate: *which rustling forests overhang.*

A firm-rooted forest, the floods overshadow.
There ever at night one an ill-meaning portent
A fire-flood may see; 'mong children of men   45
None liveth so wise that wot of the bottom;
Though harassed by hounds the heath-stepper seek for,
 Even the hounded deer will not seek refuge in these uncanny
 regions.
Fly to the forest, firm-antlered he-deer,
Spurred from afar, his spirit he yieldeth,
His life on the shore, ere in he will venture   50
To cover his head. Uncanny the place is:
Thence upward ascendeth the surging of waters,
Wan to the welkin, when the wind is stirring
The weathers unpleasing, till the air groweth gloomy,
 To thee only can I look for assistance.
And the heavens lower. Now is help to be gotten   55
From thee and thee only! The abode thou know'st not,
The dangerous place where thou'rt able to meet with
The sin-laden hero: seek if thou darest!
For the feud I will fully fee thee with money,
With old-time treasure, as erstwhile I did thee,   60
With well-twisted jewels, if away thou shalt get thee.'

XXII.

Beowulf Seeks Grendel's Mother

Beowulf answered, Ecgtheow's son:
>Beowulf exhorts the old king to arouse himself for action.

'Grieve not, O wise one! for each it is better,
His friend to avenge than with vehemence wail him;
Each of us must the end-day abide of
His earthly existence; who is able accomplish   5
Glory ere death! To battle-thane noble
Lifeless lying, 'tis at last most fitting.
Arise, O king, quick let us hasten
To look at the footprint of the kinsman of Grendel!
I promise thee this now: to his place he'll escape not,   10
To embrace of the earth, nor to mountainous forest,
Nor to depths of the ocean, wherever he wanders.
Practice thou now patient endurance
Of each of thy sorrows, as I hope for thee soothly!'

>Hrothgar rouses himself. His horse is brought.

Then up sprang the old one, the All-Wielder
    thanked he,   15
Ruler Almighty, that the man had outspoken.
Then for Hrothgar a war-horse was decked with a bridle,
Curly-maned courser. The clever folk-leader

They start on the track of the female monster.

Stately proceeded: stepped then an earl-troop
Of linden-wood bearers. Her footprints were seen then   20
Widely in wood-paths, her way o'er the bottoms,
Where she faraway fared o'er fen-country murky,
Bore away breathless the best of retainers
Who pondered with Hrothgar the welfare of country.
The son of the athelings then went o'er the stony,   25
Declivitous cliffs, the close-covered passes,
Narrow passages, paths unfrequented,
Nesses abrupt, nicker-haunts many;
One of a few of wise-mooded heroes,
He onward advanced to view the surroundings,   30
Till he found unawares woods of the mountain
O'er hoar-stones hanging, holt-wood unjoyful;
The water stood under, welling and gory.
'Twas irksome in spirit to all of the Danemen,
Friends of the Scyldings, to many a liegeman   35

The sight of Æschere's head causes them great sorrow.

Sad to be suffered, a sorrow unlittle
To each of the earlmen, when to Æschere's head they
Came on the cliff. The current was seething
With blood and with gore (the troopers gazed on it).
The horn anon sang the battle-song ready.   40
The troop were all seated; they saw 'long the water then

The water is filled with serpents and sea-dragons.

Many a serpent, mere-dragons wondrous
Trying the waters, nickers a-lying
On the cliffs of the nesses, which at noonday full often
Go on the sea-deeps their sorrowful journey,   45
Wild-beasts and wormkind; away then they hastened

One of them is killed by Beowulf.

Hot-mooded, hateful, they heard the great clamor,
The war-trumpet winding. One did the Geat-prince

Sunder from earth-joys, with arrow from bowstring,
From his sea-struggle tore him, that the trusty
    war-missile   50

       The dead beast is a poor swimmer

Pierced to his vitals; he proved in the currents
Less doughty at swimming whom death had offcarried.
Soon in the waters the wonderful swimmer
Was straitened most sorely with sword-pointed boar-spears,
Pressed in the battle and pulled to the cliff-edge;   55
The liegemen then looked on the loath-fashioned stranger.

       Beowulf prepares for a struggle with the monster.

Beowulf donned then his battle-equipments,
Cared little for life; inlaid and most ample,
The hand-woven corslet which could cover his body,
Must the wave-deeps explore, that war might be
    powerless   60
To harm the great hero, and the hating one's grasp might
Not peril his safety; his head was protected
By the light-flashing helmet that should mix with the bottoms,
Trying the eddies, treasure-emblazoned,
Encircled with jewels, as in seasons long past   65
The weapon-smith worked it, wondrously made it,
With swine-bodies fashioned it, that thenceforward no longer
Brand might bite it, and battle-sword hurt it.
And that was not least of helpers in prowess

       He has Unferth's sword in his hand.

That Hrothgar's spokesman had lent him when
    straitened;   70
And the hilted hand-sword was Hrunting entitled,
Old and most excellent 'mong all of the treasures;
Its blade was of iron, blotted with poison,
Hardened with gore; it failed not in battle
Any hero under heaven in hand who it brandished,   75
Who ventured to take the terrible journeys,
The battle-field sought; not the earliest occasion

That deeds of daring 'twas destined to 'complish.
>   Unferth has little use for swords.
Ecglaf's kinsman minded not soothly,
Exulting in strength, what erst he had spoken   80
Drunken with wine, when the weapon he lent to
A sword-hero bolder; himself did not venture
'Neath the strife of the currents his life to endanger,
To fame-deeds perform; there he forfeited glory,
Repute for his strength. Not so with the other   85
When he clad in his corslet had equipped him for battle.

XXIII.

Beowulf's Fight with Grendel's Mother

Beowulf makes a parting speech to Hrothgar.
Beowulf spake, Ecgtheow's son:
'Recall now, oh, famous kinsman of Healfdene,
Prince very prudent, now to part I am ready,
Gold-friend of earlmen, what erst we agreed on,
    If I fail, act as a kind liegelord to my thanes,
Should I lay down my life in lending thee assistance,   5
When my earth-joys were over, thou wouldst evermore
    serve me
In stead of a father; my faithful thanemen,
My trusty retainers, protect thou and care for,
Fall I in battle: and, Hrothgar belovèd,
    and send Higelac the jewels thou hast given me.
Send unto Higelac the high-valued jewels   10
Thou to me hast allotted. The lord of the Geatmen
May perceive from the gold, the Hrethling may see it
    I should like my king to know how generous a lord I found
    thee to be.
When he looks on the jewels, that a gem-giver found I
Good over-measure, enjoyed him while able.
And the ancient heirloom Unferth permit thou,   15

The famed one to have, the heavy-sword splendid[1]
The hard-edgèd weapon; with Hrunting to aid me,
I shall gain me glory, or grim-death shall take me.'

> Beowulf is eager for the fray.

The atheling of Geatmen uttered these words and
Heroic did hasten, not any rejoinder   20
Was willing to wait for; the wave-current swallowed

> He is a whole day reaching the bottom of the sea.

The doughty-in-battle. Then a day's-length elapsed ere
He was able to see the sea at its bottom.
Early she found then who fifty of winters
The course of the currents kept in her fury,   25
Grisly and greedy, that the grim one's dominion

> Grendel's mother knows that some one has reached her
> domains.

Some one of men from above was exploring.
Forth did she grab them, grappled the warrior
With horrible clutches; yet no sooner she injured
His body unscathèd: the burnie out-guarded,   30
That she proved but powerless to pierce through the armor,
The limb-mail locked, with loath-grabbing fingers.
The sea-wolf bare then, when bottomward came she,

> She grabs him, and bears him to her den.

The ring-prince homeward, that he after was powerless
(He had daring to do it) to deal with his weapons,   35
But many a mere-beast tormented him swimming,

> Sea-monsters bite and strike him.

Flood-beasts no few with fierce-biting tusks did
Break through his burnie, the brave one pursued they.
The earl then discovered he was down in some cavern
Where no water whatever anywise harmed him,   40
And the clutch of the current could come not anear him,

---

[1] Kl. emends 'wæl-sweord.' The half-line would then read, '*the battle-sword splendid*.'—For 'heard-ecg' in next half-verse, see note to 20 39 above.

Since the roofed-hall prevented; brightness a-gleaming
Fire-light he saw, flashing resplendent.
The good one saw then the sea-bottom's monster,

> Beowulf attacks the mother of Grendel.

The mighty mere-woman; he made a great onset   45
With weapon-of-battle, his hand not desisted
From striking, that war-blade struck on her head then
A battle-song greedy. The stranger perceived then

> The sword will not bite.

The sword would not bite, her life would not injure,
But the falchion failed the folk-prince when straitened: 50
Erst had it often onsets encountered,
Oft cloven the helmet, the fated one's armor:
'Twas the first time that ever the excellent jewel
Had failed of its fame. Firm-mooded after,
Not heedless of valor, but mindful of glory,   55
Was Higelac's kinsman; the hero-chief angry
Cast then his carved-sword covered with jewels
That it lay on the earth, hard and steel-pointed;

> The hero throws down all weapons, and again trusts to his
> hand-grip.

He hoped in his strength, his hand-grapple sturdy.
So any must act whenever he thinketh   60
To gain him in battle glory unending,
And is reckless of living. The lord of the War-Geats
(He shrank not from battle) seized by the shoulder[2]
The mother of Grendel; then mighty in struggle
Swung he his enemy, since his anger was kindled,   65
That she fell to the floor. With furious grapple

> Beowulf falls.

She gave him requital[3] early thereafter,

---

[2] Sw., R., and t.B. suggest 'feaxe' for 'eaxle' (1538) and render: *Seized by the hair.*

[3] If 'hand-léan' be accepted (as the MS. has it), the line will read: *She hand-reward gave him early thereafter.*

And stretched out to grab him; the strongest of warriors
Faint-mooded stumbled, till he fell in his traces,

> The monster sits on him with drawn sword.

Foot-going champion. Then she sat on the hall-guest   70
And wielded her war-knife wide-bladed, flashing,
For her son would take vengeance, her one only bairn.

> His armor saves his life.

His breast-armor woven bode on his shoulder;
It guarded his life, the entrance defended
'Gainst sword-point and edges. Ecgtheow's son there   75
Had fatally journeyed, champion of Geatmen,
In the arms of the ocean, had the armor not given,
Close-woven corslet, comfort and succor,

> God arranged for his escape.

And had God most holy not awarded the victory,
All-knowing Lord; easily did heaven's   80
Ruler most righteous arrange it with justice;[4]
Uprose he erect ready for battle.

---

[4] Sw. and S. change H.-So.'s semicolon (v. 1557) to a comma, and translate: *The Ruler of Heaven arranged it in justice easily, after he arose again.*

XXIV.

Beowulf is Double-Conqueror

Beowulf grasps a giant-sword,

Then he saw 'mid the war-gems a weapon of victory,
An ancient giant-sword, of edges a-doughty,
Glory of warriors: of weapons 'twas choicest,
Only 'twas larger than any man else was
Able to bear to the battle-encounter,   5
The good and splendid work of the giants.
He grasped then the sword-hilt, knight of the Scyldings,
Bold and battle-grim, brandished his ring-sword,
Hopeless of living, hotly he smote her,
That the fiend-woman's neck firmly it grappled,   10

and fells the female monster.

Broke through her bone-joints, the bill fully pierced her
Fate-cursèd body, she fell to the ground then:
The hand-sword was bloody, the hero exulted.
The brand was brilliant, brightly it glimmered,
Just as from heaven gemlike shineth   15
The torch of the firmament. He glanced 'long the building,
And turned by the wall then, Higelac's vassal
Raging and wrathful raised his battle-sword
Strong by the handle. The edge was not useless
To the hero-in-battle, but he speedily wished to   20

Give Grendel requital for the many assaults he
Had worked on the West-Danes not once, but often,
When he slew in slumber the subjects of Hrothgar,
Swallowed down fifteen sleeping retainers
Of the folk of the Danemen, and fully as many   25
Carried away, a horrible prey.
He gave him requital, grim-raging champion,

> Beowulf sees the body of Grendel, and cuts off his head.

When he saw on his rest-place weary of conflict
Grendel lying, of life-joys bereavèd,
As the battle at Heorot erstwhile had scathed him;   30
His body far bounded, a blow when he suffered,
Death having seized him, sword-smiting heavy,
And he cut off his head then. Early this noticed
The clever carles who as comrades of Hrothgar

> The waters are gory.

Gazed on the sea-deeps, that the surging wave-currents 35
Were mightily mingled, the mere-flood was gory:
Of the good one the gray-haired together held converse,

> Beowulf is given up for dead.

The hoary of head, that they hoped not to see again
The atheling ever, that exulting in victory
He'd return there to visit the distinguished folk-ruler: 40
Then many concluded the mere-wolf had killed him.[1]

---

[1] 'Þæs monige gewearð' (1599) and 'hafað þæs geworden' (2027).—In a
paper published some years ago in one of the Johns Hopkins University
circulars, I tried to throw upon these two long-doubtful passages some light
derived from a study of like passages in Alfred's prose.—The impersonal
verb 'geweorðan,' with an accus. of the person, and a þæt-clause is used
several times with the meaning 'agree.' See Orosius (Sweet's ed.) 1787;
20434; 20828; 21015; 28020. In the two *Beowulf* passages, the þæt-clause
is anticipated by 'þæs,' which is clearly a gen. of the thing agreed on.

The first passage (v. 1599 (b)—1600) I translate literally: *Then many
agreed upon this (namely), that the sea-wolf had killed him.*

The second passage (v. 2025 (b)—2027): *She is promised . . .; to this the
friend of the Scyldings has agreed, etc.* By emending 'is' instead of 'wæs'
(2025), the tenses will be brought into perfect harmony.

The ninth hour came then. From the ness-edge departed
The bold-mooded Scyldings; the gold-friend of heroes
Homeward betook him. The strangers sat down then
Soul-sick, sorrowful, the sea-waves regarding: 45
They wished and yet weened not their well-loved friend-lord

> The giant-sword melts.

To see any more. The sword-blade began then,
The blood having touched it, contracting and shriveling
With battle-icicles; 'twas a wonderful marvel
That it melted entirely, likest to ice when   50
The Father unbindeth the bond of the frost and
Unwindeth the wave-bands, He who wieldeth dominion
Of times and of tides: a truth-firm Creator.
Nor took he of jewels more in the dwelling,
Lord of the Weders, though they lay all around him,   55
Than the head and the handle handsome with jewels;
The brand early melted, burnt was the weapon:[2]
So hot was the blood, the strange-spirit poisonous

> The hero swims back to the realms of day.

That in it did perish. He early swam off then
Who had bided in combat the carnage of haters,   60
Went up through the ocean; the eddies were cleansèd,
The spacious expanses, when the spirit from farland
His life put aside and this short-lived existence.
The seamen's defender came swimming to land then

In v. 1997 ff. this same idiom occurs, and was noticed in B.'s great article on *Beowulf*, which appeared about the time I published my reading of 1599 and 2027. Translate 1997 then: *Wouldst let the South-Danes themselves decide about their struggle with Grendel.* Here 'Súð-Dene' is accus. of person, and 'gúðe' is gen. of thing agreed on.

With such collateral support as that afforded by B. (P. and B. XII. 97), I have no hesitation in departing from H.-So., my usual guide.

The idiom above treated runs through A.-S., Old Saxon, and other Teutonic languages, and should be noticed in the lexicons.

[2] 'Bróden-mæl' is regarded by most scholars as meaning a damaskeened sword. Translate: *The damaskeened sword burned up.* Cf. 25 16 and note.

Doughty of spirit, rejoiced in his sea-gift,   65
The bulky burden which he bore in his keeping.
The excellent vassals advanced then to meet him,
To God they were grateful, were glad in their chieftain,
That to see him safe and sound was granted them.
From the high-minded hero, then, helmet and burnie   70
Were speedily loosened: the ocean was putrid,
The water 'neath welkin weltered with gore.
Forth did they fare, then, their footsteps retracing,
Merry and mirthful, measured the earth-way,
The highway familiar: men very daring[3]   75
Bare then the head from the sea-cliff, burdening
Each of the earlmen, excellent-valiant.

       It takes four men to carry Grendel's head on a spear.

Four of them had to carry with labor
The head of Grendel to the high towering gold-hall
Upstuck on the spear, till fourteen most-valiant   80
And battle-brave Geatmen came there going
Straight to the palace: the prince of the people
Measured the mead-ways, their mood-brave companion.
The atheling of earlmen entered the building,
Deed-valiant man, adorned with distinction,   85
Doughty shield-warrior, to address King Hrothgar:
Then hung by the hair, the head of Grendel
Was borne to the building, where beer-thanes were drinking,
Loth before earlmen and eke 'fore the lady:
The warriors beheld then a wonderful sight.   90

---

[3] 'Cyning-balde' (1635) is the much-disputed reading of K. and Th. To
render this, '*nobly bold*,' '*excellently bold*,' have been suggested. B. would
read 'cyning-holde' (cf. 290), and render: *Men well-disposed towards the
king carried the head, etc.* 'Cynebealde,' says t.B., endorsing Gr.

XXV.

Beowulf Brings his Trophies—Hrothgar's Gratitude

Beowulf relates his last exploit.

Beowulf spake, offspring of Ecgtheow:
'Lo! we blithely have brought thee, bairn of Healfdene,
Prince of the Scyldings, these presents from ocean
Which thine eye looketh on, for an emblem of glory.
I came off alive from this, narrowly 'scaping: 5
In war 'neath the water the work with great pains I
Performed, and the fight had been finished quite nearly,
Had God not defended me. I failed in the battle
Aught to accomplish, aided by Hrunting,
Though that weapon was worthy, but the Wielder of
    earth-folk   10

God was fighting with me.

Gave me willingly to see on the wall a
Heavy old hand-sword hanging in splendor
(He guided most often the lorn and the friendless),
That I swung as a weapon. The wards of the house then
I killed in the conflict (when occasion was given me).   15
Then the battle-sword burned, the brand that was lifted,[1]

---

[1] Or rather, perhaps, '*the inlaid, or damaskeened weapon.*' Cf. 24 57 and note.

As the blood-current sprang, hottest of war-sweats;
Seizing the hilt, from my foes I offbore it;
I avenged as I ought to their acts of malignity,
The murder of Danemen. I then make thee this
    promise, 20
    Heorot is freed from monsters.
Thou'lt be able in Heorot careless to slumber
With thy throng of heroes and the thanes of thy people
Every and each, of greater and lesser,
And thou needest not fear for them from the selfsame direction
As thou formerly fearedst, oh, folk-lord of Scyldings, 25
End-day for earlmen.' To the age-hoary man then,
    The famous sword is presented to Hrothgar.
The gray-haired chieftain, the gold-fashioned sword-hilt,
Old-work of giants, was thereupon given;
Since the fall of the fiends, it fell to the keeping
Of the wielder of Danemen, the wonder-smith's labor, 30
And the bad-mooded being abandoned this world then,
Opponent of God, victim of murder,
And also his mother; it went to the keeping
Of the best of the world-kings, where waters encircle,
Who the scot divided in Scylding dominion. 35
    Hrothgar looks closely at the old sword.
Hrothgar discoursed, the hilt he regarded,
The ancient heirloom where an old-time contention's
Beginning was graven: the gurgling currents,
The flood slew thereafter the race of the giants,
They had proved themselves daring: that people was
    loth to 40
    It had belonged to a race hateful to God.
The Lord everlasting, through lash of the billows
The Father gave them final requital.
So in letters of rune on the clasp of the handle
Gleaming and golden, 'twas graven exactly,

Set forth and said, whom that sword had been made
    for,   45
Finest of irons, who first it was wrought for,
Wreathed at its handle and gleaming with serpents.
The wise one then said (silent they all were)

        Hrothgar praises Beowulf.

Son of old Healfdene: 'He may say unrefuted
Who performs 'mid the folk-men fairness and truth   50
(The hoary old ruler remembers the past),
That better by birth is this bairn of the nobles!
Thy fame is extended through far-away countries,
Good friend Beowulf, o'er all of the races,
Thou holdest all firmly, hero-like strength with   55
Prudence of spirit. I'll prove myself grateful
As before we agreed on; thou granted for long shalt
Become a great comfort to kinsmen and comrades,

        Heremod's career is again contrasted with Beowulf's.

A help unto heroes. Heremod became not
Such to the Scyldings, successors of Ecgwela;   60
He grew not to please them, but grievous destruction,
And diresome death-woes to Danemen attracted;
He slew in anger his table-companions,
Trustworthy counsellors, till he turned off lonely
From world-joys away, wide-famous ruler: 65
Though high-ruling heaven in hero-strength raised him,
In might exalted him, o'er men of all nations
Made him supreme, yet a murderous spirit
Grew in his bosom: he gave then no ring-gems

        A wretched failure of a king, to give no jewels to his retainers.

To the Danes after custom; endured he unjoyful   70
Standing the straits from strife that was raging,
Longsome folk-sorrow. Learn then from this,
Lay hold of virtue! Though laden with winters,
I have sung thee these measures. 'Tis a marvel to tell it,

        Hrothgar moralizes.

How all-ruling God from greatness of spirit   75
Giveth wisdom to children of men,
Manor and earlship: all things He ruleth.
He often permitteth the mood-thought of man of
The illustrious lineage to lean to possessions,
Allows him earthly delights at his manor,   80
A high-burg of heroes to hold in his keeping,
Maketh portions of earth-folk hear him,
And a wide-reaching kingdom so that, wisdom failing him,
He himself is unable to reckon its boundaries;
He liveth in luxury, little debars him,   85
Nor sickness nor age, no treachery-sorrow
Becloudeth his spirit, conflict nowhere,
No sword-hate, appeareth, but all of the world doth
Wend as he wisheth; the worse he knoweth not,
Till arrant arrogance inward pervading,   90
Waxeth and springeth, when the warder is sleeping,
The guard of the soul: with sorrows encompassed,
Too sound is his slumber, the slayer is near him,
Who with bow and arrow aimeth in malice.

XXVI.

Hrothgar Moralizes—Rest after Labor

A wounded spirit.
'Then bruised in his bosom he with bitter-toothed
    missile
Is hurt 'neath his helmet: from harmful pollution
He is powerless to shield him by the wonderful mandates
Of the loath-cursèd spirit; what too long he hath holden
Him seemeth too small, savage he hoardeth,   5
Nor boastfully giveth gold-plated rings,[1]
The fate of the future flouts and forgetteth
Since God had erst given him greatness no little,
Wielder of Glory. His end-day anear,
It afterward happens that the bodily-dwelling   10
Fleetingly fadeth, falls into ruins;
Another lays hold who doleth the ornaments,
The nobleman's jewels, nothing lamenting,
Heedeth no terror. Oh, Beowulf dear,
Best of the heroes, from bale-strife defend thee,   15
And choose thee the better, counsels eternal;

---

[1] K. says '*proudly giveth.*'—Gr. says, '*And gives no gold-plated rings, in order to incite the recipient to boastfulness.*'—B. suggests 'gyld' for 'gylp,' and renders: *And gives no beaten rings for reward.*

> Be not over proud: life is fleeting, and its strength soon
> wasteth away.

Beware of arrogance, world-famous champion!
But a little-while lasts thy life-vigor's fulness;
'Twill after hap early, that illness or sword-edge
Shall part thee from strength, or the grasp of the fire,   20
Or the wave of the current, or clutch of the edges,
Or flight of the war-spear, or age with its horrors,
Or thine eyes' bright flashing shall fade into darkness:
'Twill happen full early, excellent hero,

> Hrothgar gives an account of his reign.

That death shall subdue thee. So the Danes a half-century 25
I held under heaven, helped them in struggles
'Gainst many a race in middle-earth's regions,
With ash-wood and edges, that enemies none
On earth molested me. Lo! offsetting change, now,

> Sorrow after joy.

Came to my manor, grief after joyance,   30
When Grendel became my constant visitor,
Inveterate hater: I from that malice
Continually travailed with trouble no little.
Thanks be to God that I gained in my lifetime,
To the Lord everlasting, to look on the gory   35
Head with mine eyes, after long-lasting sorrow!
Go to the bench now, battle-adornèd
Joy in the feasting: of jewels in common
We'll meet with many when morning appeareth.'
The Geatman was gladsome, ganged he immediately   40
To go to the bench, as the clever one bade him.
Then again as before were the famous-for-prowess,
Hall-inhabiters, handsomely banqueted,
Feasted anew. The night-veil fell then
Dark o'er the warriors. The courtiers rose then;   45
The gray-haired was anxious to go to his slumbers,
The hoary old Scylding. Hankered the Geatman,

Beowulf is fagged, and seeks rest.

The champion doughty, greatly, to rest him:
An earlman early outward did lead him,
Fagged from his faring, from far-country springing,   50
Who for etiquette's sake all of a liegeman's
Needs regarded, such as seamen at that time
Were bounden to feel. The big-hearted rested;
The building uptowered, spacious and gilded,
The guest within slumbered, till the sable-clad raven   55
Blithely foreboded the beacon of heaven.
Then the bright-shining sun o'er the bottoms came going;[2]
The warriors hastened, the heads of the peoples
Were ready to go again to their peoples,

The Geats prepare to leave Dane-land.

The high-mooded farer would faraway thenceward   60
Look for his vessel. The valiant one bade then,[3]

Unferth asks Beowulf to accept his sword as a gift. Beowulf
thanks him.

Offspring of Ecglaf, off to bear Hrunting,
To take his weapon, his well-beloved iron;
He him thanked for the gift, saying good he accounted
The war-friend and mighty, nor chid he with words then 65
The blade of the brand: 'twas a brave-mooded hero.
When the warriors were ready, arrayed in their trappings,
The atheling dear to the Danemen advanced then
On to the dais, where the other was sitting,
Grim-mooded hero, greeted King Hrothgar.   70

---

[2] If S.'s emendation be accepted, v. 57 will read: *Then came the light, going
bright after darkness: the warriors, etc.*
[3] As the passage stands in H.-So., Unferth presents Beowulf with the sword
Hrunting, and B. thanks him for the gift. If, however, the suggestions of
Grdtvg. and M. be accepted, the passage will read: *Then the brave one* (i.e.
*Beowulf) commanded that Hrunting be borne to the son of Ecglaf (Unferth),
bade him take his sword, his dear weapon; he (B.) thanked him (U.) for the
loan, etc.*

XXVII.

Sorrow at Parting

Beowulf's farewell.
Beowulf spake, Ecgtheow's offspring:
'We men of the water wish to declare now
Fared from far-lands, we're firmly determined
To seek King Higelac. Here have we fitly
Been welcomed and feasted, as heart would desire it;   5
Good was the greeting. If greater affection
I am anywise able ever on earth to
Gain at thy hands, ruler of heroes,
Than yet I have done, I shall quickly be ready
I shall be ever ready to aid thee.
For combat and conflict. O'er the course of the waters   10
Learn I that neighbors alarm thee with terror,
As haters did whilom, I hither will bring thee
For help unto heroes henchmen by thousands.
My liegelord will encourage me in aiding thee.
I know as to Higelac, the lord of the Geatmen,
Though young in years, he yet will permit me,   15
By words and by works, ward of the people,
Fully to furnish thee forces and bear thee
My lance to relieve thee, if liegemen shall fail thee,
And help of my hand-strength; if Hrethric be treating,

Bairn of the king, at the court of the Geatmen,   20
He thereat may find him friends in abundance:
Faraway countries he were better to seek for
Who trusts in himself.' Hrothgar discoursed then,
Making rejoinder: 'These words thou hast uttered
All-knowing God hath given thy spirit!   25
    O Beowulf, thou art wise beyond thy years.
Ne'er heard I an earlman thus early in life
More clever in speaking: thou'rt cautious of spirit,
Mighty of muscle, in mouth-answers prudent.
I count on the hope that, happen it ever
That missile shall rob thee of Hrethel's descendant,   30
Edge-horrid battle, and illness or weapon
Deprive thee of prince, of people's protector,
    Should Higelac die, the Geats could find no better successor
    than thou wouldst make.
And life thou yet holdest, the Sea-Geats will never
Find a more fitting folk-lord to choose them,
Gem-ward of heroes, than *thou* mightest prove thee,   35
If the kingdom of kinsmen thou carest to govern.
Thy mood-spirit likes me the longer the better,
Beowulf dear: thou hast brought it to pass that
To both these peoples peace shall be common,
    Thou hast healed the ancient breach between our races.
To Geat-folk and Danemen, the strife be suspended,   40
The secret assailings they suffered in yore-days;
And also that jewels be shared while I govern
The wide-stretching kingdom, and that many shall visit
Others o'er the ocean with excellent gift-gems:
The ring-adorned bark shall bring o'er the currents   45
Presents and love-gifts. This people I know
Tow'rd foeman and friend firmly established,[1]

---

[1] For 'geworhte,' the crux of this passage, B. proposes 'geþóhte,' rendering:
*I know this people with firm thought every way blameless towards foe and
friends.*

After ancient etiquette everywise blameless.'
Then the warden of earlmen gave him still farther,
    Parting gifts
Kinsman of Healfdene, a dozen of jewels,   50
Bade him safely seek with the presents
His well-beloved people, early returning.
      Hrothgar kisses Beowulf, and weeps.
Then the noble-born king kissed the distinguished,
Dear-lovèd liegeman, the Dane-prince saluted him,
And claspèd his neck; tears from him fell,   55
From the gray-headed man: he two things expected,
Agèd and reverend, but rather the second,
[2]That bold in council they'd meet thereafter.
The man was so dear that he failed to suppress the
Emotions that moved him, but in mood-fetters fastened 60
     The old king is deeply grieved to part with his benefactor.
The long-famous hero longeth in secret
Deep in his spirit for the dear-beloved man
Though not a blood-kinsman. Beowulf thenceward,
Gold-splendid warrior, walked o'er the meadows
Exulting in treasure: the sea-going vessel   65
Riding at anchor awaited its owner.
As they pressed on their way then, the present of Hrothgar
    Giving liberally is the true proof of kingship.
Was frequently referred to: a folk-king indeed that
Everyway blameless, till age did debar him
The joys of his might, which hath many oft injured.   70

[2] S. and B. emend so as to negative the verb 'meet.' 'Why should Hrothgar weep if he expects to meet Beowulf again?' both these scholars ask. But the weeping is mentioned before the 'expectations': the tears may have been due to many emotions, especially gratitude, struggling for expression.

XXVIII.

The Homeward Journey—The Two Queens

Then the band of very valiant retainers
Came to the current; they were clad all in armor,

> The coast-guard again.

In link-woven burnies. The land-warder noticed
The return of the earlmen, as he erstwhile had seen them;
Nowise with insult he greeted the strangers   5
From the naze of the cliff, but rode on to meet them;
Said the bright-armored visitors[1] vesselward traveled
Welcome to Weders. The wide-bosomed craft then
Lay on the sand, laden with armor,
With horses and jewels, the ring-stemmèd sailer: 10
The mast uptowered o'er the treasure of Hrothgar.

> Beowulf gives the guard a handsome sword.

To the boat-ward a gold-bound brand he presented,
That he was afterwards honored on the ale-bench more highly
As the heirloom's owner. [2]Set he out on his vessel,

---

[1] For 'scawan' (1896), 'scaðan' has been proposed. Accepting this, we may render: *He said the bright-armored warriors were going to their vessel, welcome, etc.* (Cf. 1804.)

[2] R. suggests, 'Gewát him on naca,' and renders: *The vessel set out, to drive on the sea, the Dane-country left.* 'On' bears the alliteration; cf. 'on hafu'

To drive on the deep, Dane-country left he.   15
Along by the mast then a sea-garment fluttered,
A rope-fastened sail. The sea-boat resounded,
The wind o'er the waters the wave-floater nowise
Kept from its journey; the sea-goer traveled,
The foamy-necked floated forth o'er the currents,   20
The well-fashioned vessel o'er the ways of the ocean,
> The Geats see their own land again.
Till they came within sight of the cliffs of the Geatmen,
The well-known headlands. The wave-goer hastened
Driven by breezes, stood on the shore.
> The port-warden is anxiously looking for them.
Prompt at the ocean, the port-ward was ready,   25
Who long in the past outlooked in the distance,[3]
At water's-edge waiting well-lovèd heroes;
He bound to the bank then the broad-bosomed vessel
Fast in its fetters, lest the force of the waters
Should be able to injure the ocean-wood winsome.   30
Bade he up then take the treasure of princes,
Plate-gold and fretwork; not far was it thence
To go off in search of the giver of jewels:
Hrethel's son Higelac at home there remaineth,[4]
Himself with his comrades close to the sea-coast.   35
The building was splendid, the king heroic,
Great in his hall, Hygd very young was,
> Hygd, the noble queen of Higelac, lavish of gifts.

(2524). This has some advantages over the H.-So. reading; viz. (1) It adds nothing to the text; (2) it makes 'naca' the subject, and thus brings the passage into keeping with the context, where the poet has exhausted his vocabulary in detailing the actions of the vessel.—B.'s emendation (cf. P. and B. XII. 97) is violent.

[3] B. translates: *Who for a long time, ready at the coast, had looked out into the distance eagerly for the dear men.* This changes the syntax of 'léofra manna.'

[4] For 'wunað' (v. 1924) several eminent critics suggest 'wunade' (=remained). This makes the passage much clearer.

Fine-mooded, clever, though few were the winters
That the daughter of Hæreth had dwelt in the borough;
But she nowise was cringing nor niggard of presents,   40
Of ornaments rare, to the race of the Geatmen.

    Offa's consort, Thrytho, is contrasted with Hygd.

Thrytho nursed anger, excellent[5] folk-queen,
Hot-burning hatred: no hero whatever
'Mong household companions, her husband excepted

    She is a terror to all save her husband.

Dared to adventure to look at the woman   45
With eyes in the daytime;[6] but he knew that death-chains
Hand-wreathed were wrought him: early thereafter,
When the hand-strife was over, edges were ready,
That fierce-raging sword-point had to force a decision,
Murder-bale show. Such no womanly custom   50
For a lady to practise, though lovely her person,
That a weaver-of-peace, on pretence of anger
A belovèd liegeman of life should deprive.
Soothly this hindered Heming's kinsman;
Other ale-drinking earlmen asserted   55
That fearful folk-sorrows fewer she wrought them,
Treacherous doings, since first she was given
Adorned with gold to the war-hero youthful,
For her origin honored, when Offa's great palace
O'er the fallow flood by her father's instructions   60
She sought on her journey, where she afterwards fully,
Famed for her virtue, her fate on the king's-seat
Enjoyed in her lifetime, love did she hold with
The ruler of heroes, the best, it is told me,
Of all of the earthmen that oceans encompass,   65

---

[5] Why should such a woman be described as an 'excellent' queen? C.
suggests 'frécnu' = dangerous, bold.
[6] For 'an dæges' various readings have been offered. If 'and-éges' be
accepted, the sentence will read: *No hero . . . dared look upon her, eye to
eye.* If 'án-dæges' be adopted, translate: *Dared look upon her the whole day.*

Of earl-kindreds endless; hence Offa was famous
Far and widely, by gifts and by battles,
Spear-valiant hero; the home of his fathers
He governed with wisdom, whence Eomær did issue
For help unto heroes, Heming's kinsman,   70
Grandson of Garmund, great in encounters.

XXIX.

Beowulf and Higelac

Then the brave one departed, his band along with him,
> Beowulf and his party seek Higelac.

Seeking the sea-shore, the sea-marches treading,
The wide-stretching shores. The world-candle glimmered,
The sun from the southward; they proceeded then
    onward,
Early arriving where they heard that the troop-lord,   5
Ongentheow's slayer, excellent, youthful
Folk-prince and warrior was distributing jewels,
Close in his castle. The coming of Beowulf
Was announced in a message quickly to Higelac,
That the folk-troop's defender forth to the palace   10
The linden-companion alive was advancing,
Secure from the combat courtward a-going.
The building was early inward made ready
For the foot-going guests as the good one had ordered.
> Beowulf sits by his liegelord.

He sat by the man then who had lived through the
    struggle,   15
Kinsman by kinsman, when the king of the people
Had in lordly language saluted the dear one,

Queen Hygd receives the heroes.

In words that were formal. The daughter of Hæreth
Coursed through the building, carrying mead-cups:[1]
She loved the retainers, tendered the beakers   20
To the high-minded Geatmen. Higelac 'gan then

Higelac is greatly interested in Beowulf's adventures.

Pleasantly plying his companion with questions
In the high-towering palace. A curious interest
Tormented his spirit, what meaning to see in
The Sea-Geats' adventures: 'Beowulf worthy,   25

Give an account of thy adventures, Beowulf dear.

How throve your journeying, when thou thoughtest
     suddenly
Far o'er the salt-streams to seek an encounter,
A battle at Heorot? Hast bettered for Hrothgar,
The famous folk-leader, his far-published sorrows
Any at all? In agony-billows   30

My suspense has been great.

I mused upon torture, distrusted the journey
Of the belovèd liegeman; I long time did pray thee
By no means to seek out the murderous spirit,
To suffer the South-Danes themselves to decide on[2]
Grappling with Grendel. To God I am thankful   35
To be suffered to see thee safe from thy journey.'

Beowulf narrates his adventures.

Beowulf answered, bairn of old Ecgtheow:
''Tis hidden by no means, Higelac chieftain,
From many of men, the meeting so famous,
What mournful moments of me and of Grendel   40
Were passed in the place where he pressing affliction
On the Victory-Scyldings scathefully brought,

---

[1] 'Meodu-scencum' (1981) some would render 'with mead-pourers.'
Translate then: *The daughter of Hæreth went through the building
accompanied by mead-pourers.*
[2] See my note to 1599, supra, and B. in P. and B. XII. 97.

Anguish forever; that all I avengèd,
So that any under heaven of the kinsmen of Grendel

> Grendel's kindred have no cause to boast.

Needeth not boast of that cry-in-the-morning,   45
Who longest liveth of the loth-going kindred,[3]
Encompassed by moorland. I came in my journey
To the royal ring-hall, Hrothgar to greet there:

> Hrothgar received me very cordially.

Soon did the famous scion of Healfdene,
When he understood fully the spirit that led me,   50
Assign me a seat with the son of his bosom.
The troop was in joyance; mead-glee greater
'Neath arch of the ether not ever beheld I

> The queen also showed up no little honor.

'Mid hall-building holders. The highly-famed queen,
Peace-tie of peoples, oft passed through the building,   55
Cheered the young troopers; she oft tendered a hero
A beautiful ring-band, ere she went to her sitting.

> Hrothgar's lovely daughter.

Oft the daughter of Hrothgar in view of the courtiers
To the earls at the end the ale-vessel carried,
Whom Freaware I heard then hall-sitters title,   60
When nail-adorned jewels she gave to the heroes:

> She is betrothed to Ingeld, in order to unite the Danes and
> Heathobards.

Gold-bedecked, youthful, to the glad son of Froda
Her faith has been plighted; the friend of the Scyldings,
The guard of the kingdom, hath given his sanction,[4]
And counts it a vantage, for a part of the quarrels,   65
A portion of hatred, to pay with the woman.

---

[3] For 'fenne,' supplied by Grdtvg., B. suggests 'fácne' (cf. Jul. 350).
Accepting this, translate: *Who longest lives of the hated race, steeped in
treachery.*
[4] See note to v. 1599 above.

[5]Somewhere not rarely, when the ruler has fallen,
The life-taking lance relaxeth its fury
For a brief breathing-spell, though the bride be charming!

---

[5] This is perhaps the least understood sentence in the poem, almost every word being open to dispute. (1) The 'nó' of our text is an emendation, and is rejected by many scholars. (2) 'Seldan' is by some taken as an adv. (= *seldom*), and by others as a noun (= *page, companion*). (3) 'Léod-hryre,' some render '*fall of the people*'; others, '*fall of the prince.*' (4) 'Búgeð,' most scholars regard as the intrans. verb meaning '*bend*,' '*rest*'; but one great scholar has translated it '*shall kill.*' (5) 'Hwær,' very recently, has been attacked, 'wære' being suggested. (6) As a corollary to the above, the same critic proposes to drop 'oft' out of the text.—t.B. suggests: Oft seldan wære after léodhryre: lýtle hwíle bongár búgeð, þéah séo brýd duge = *often has a treaty been (thus) struck, after a prince had fallen: (but only) a short time is the spear (then) wont to rest, however excellent the bride may be.*

XXX.

Beowulf Narrates his Adventures
to Higelac

'It well may discomfit the prince of the Heathobards
And each of the thanemen of earls that attend him,
When he goes to the building escorting the woman,
That a noble-born Daneman the knights should be feasting:
There gleam on his person the leavings of elders   5
Hard and ring-bright, Heathobards' treasure,
While they wielded their arms, till they misled to
    the battle
Their own dear lives and belovèd companions.
He saith at the banquet who the collar beholdeth,
An ancient ash-warrior who earlmen's destruction   10
Clearly recalleth (cruel his spirit),
Sadly beginneth sounding the youthful
Thane-champion's spirit through the thoughts of his bosom,
War-grief to waken, and this word-answer speaketh:
    Ingeld is stirred up to break the truce.
'Art thou able, my friend, to know when thou seest it   15
The brand which thy father bare to the conflict
In his latest adventure, 'neath visor of helmet,
The dearly-loved iron, where Danemen did slay him,
And brave-mooded Scyldings, on the fall of the heroes,

(When vengeance was sleeping) the slaughter-place
    wielded? 20
E'en now some man of the murderer's progeny
Exulting in ornaments enters the building,
Boasts of his blood-shedding, offbeareth the jewel
Which thou shouldst wholly hold in possession!'
So he urgeth and mindeth on every occasion 25
With woe-bringing words, till waxeth the season
When thc woman's thane for the works of his father,
The bill having bitten, blood-gory sleepeth,
Fated to perish; the other one thenceward
'Scapeth alive, the land knoweth thoroughly.[1] 30
Then the oaths of the earlmen on each side are broken,
When rancors unresting are raging in Ingeld
And his wife-love waxeth less warm after sorrow.
So the Heathobards' favor not faithful I reckon,
Their part in the treaty not true to the Danemen, 35
Their friendship not fast. I further shall tell thee

    Having made these preliminary statements, I will now tell
    thee of Grendel, the monster.

More about Grendel, that thou fully mayst hear,
Ornament-giver, what afterward came from
The hand-rush of heroes. When heaven's bright jewel
O'er earthfields had glided, the stranger came raging, 40
The horrible night-fiend, us for to visit,
Where wholly unharmed the hall we were guarding.

    Hondscio fell first

To Hondscio happened a hopeless contention,
Death to the doomed one, dead he fell foremost,
Girded war-champion; to him Grendel became then, 45
To the vassal distinguished, a tooth-weaponed murderer,
The well-beloved henchman's body all swallowed.

---

[1] For 'lifigende' (2063), a mere conjecture, 'wigende' has been suggested.
The line would then read: *Escapeth by fighting, knows the land thoroughly.*

Not the earlier off empty of hand did
The bloody-toothed murderer, mindful of evils,
Wish to escape from the gold-giver's palace,　　　　50
But sturdy of strength he strove to outdo me,
Hand-ready grappled. A glove was suspended
Spacious and wondrous, in art-fetters fastened,
Which was fashioned entirely by touch of the craftman
From the dragon's skin by the devil's devices:　　　55
He down in its depths would do me unsadly
One among many, deed-doer raging,
Though sinless he saw me; not so could it happen
When I in my anger upright did stand.
'Tis too long to recount how requital I furnished　　60
For every evil to the earlmen's destroyer;

     I reflected honor upon my people.

'Twas there, my prince, that I proudly distinguished
Thy land with my labors. He left and retreated,
He lived his life a little while longer:
Yet his right-hand guarded his footstep in Heorot,　　65
And sad-mooded thence to the sea-bottom fell he,
Mournful in mind. For the might-rush of battle

     King Hrothgar lavished gifts upon me.

The friend of the Scyldings, with gold that was plated,
With ornaments many, much requited me,
When daylight had dawned, and down to the banquet　70
We had sat us together. There was chanting and joyance:
The age-stricken Scylding asked many questions
And of old-times related; oft light-ringing harp-strings,
Joy-telling wood, were touched by the brave one;
Now he uttered measures, mourning and truthful,　　75
Then the large-hearted land-king a legend of wonder
Truthfully told us. Now troubled with years

     The old king is sad over the loss of his youthful vigor.

The age-hoary warrior afterward began to
Mourn for the might that marked him in youth-days;

His breast within boiled, when burdened with winters   80
Much he remembered. From morning till night then
We joyed us therein as etiquette suffered,
Till the second night season came unto earth-folk.
Then early thereafter, the mother of Grendel

> Grendel's mother.

Was ready for vengeance, wretched she journeyed;   85
Her son had death ravished, the wrath of the Geatmen.
The horrible woman avengèd her offspring,
And with mighty mainstrength murdered a hero.

> Æschere falls a prey to her vengeance.

There the spirit of Æschere, agèd adviser,
Was ready to vanish; nor when morn had lightened   90
Were they anywise suffered to consume him with fire,
Folk of the Danemen, the death-weakened hero,
Nor the belovèd liegeman to lay on the pyre;

> She suffered not his body to be burned, but ate it.

She the corpse had offcarried in the clutch of the foeman[2]
'Neath mountain-brook's flood. To Hrothgar 'twas
  saddest   95
Of pains that ever had preyed on the chieftain;
By the life of thee the land-prince then me[3]
Besought very sadly, in sea-currents' eddies
To display my prowess, to peril my safety,
Might-deeds accomplish; much did he promise.   100

> I sought the creature in her den,

I found then the famous flood-current's cruel,
Horrible depth-warder. A while unto us two
Hand was in common; the currents were seething

---

[2] For 'fæðmum,' Gr.'s conjecture, B. proposes 'færunga.' These three half-verses would then read: *She bore off the corpse of her foe suddenly under the mountain-torrent.*

[3] The phrase 'þíne lýfe' (2132) was long rendered '*with thy (presupposed) permission.*' The verse would read: *The land-prince then sadly besought me, with thy (presupposed) permission, etc.*

With gore that was clotted, and Grendel's fierce mother's
    and hewed her head off.
Head I offhacked in the hall at the bottom   105
With huge-reaching sword-edge, hardly I wrested
My life from her clutches; not doomed was I then,
    Jewels were freely bestowed upon me.
But the warden of earlmen afterward gave me
Jewels in quantity, kinsman of Healfdene.

XXXI.

Gift-Giving is Mutual

'So the belovèd land-prince lived in decorum;
I had missed no rewards, no meeds of my prowess,
But he gave me jewels, regarding my wishes,
Healfdene his bairn; I'll bring them to thee, then,
    All my gifts I lay at thy feet.
Atheling of earlmen, offer them gladly.   5
And still unto thee is all my affection:[1]
But few of my folk-kin find I surviving
But thee, dear Higelac!' Bade he in then to carry[2]
The boar-image, banner, battle-high helmet,
Iron-gray armor, the excellent weapon,   10
    This armor I have belonged of yore to Heregar.
In song-measures said: 'This suit-for-the-battle
Hrothgar presented me, bade me expressly,
Wise-mooded atheling, thereafter to tell thee[3]

---

[1] This verse B. renders, '*Now serve I again thee alone as my gracious king.*'
[2] For 'eafor' (2153), Kl. suggests 'ealdor.' Translate then: *Bade the prince then to bear in the banner, battle-high helmet, etc.* On the other hand, W. takes 'eaforhéafodsegn' as a compound, meaning 'helmet': *He bade them bear in the helmet, battle-high helm, gray armor, etc.*
[3] The H.-So. rendering (ærest = *history, origin*; 'eft' for 'est'), though liable to objection, is perhaps the best offered. 'That I should very early tell thee

The whole of its history, said King Heregar owned it,
Dane-prince for long: yet he wished not to give then   15
The mail to his son, though dearly he loved him,
Hereward the hardy. Hold all in joyance!'
I heard that there followed hard on the jewels
Two braces of stallions of striking resemblance,
Dappled and yellow; he granted him usance   20
Of horses and treasures. So a kinsman should bear him,
No web of treachery weave for another,
Nor by cunning craftiness cause the destruction

> Higelac loves his nephew Beowulf.`

Of trusty companion. Most precious to Higelac,
The bold one in battle, was the bairn of his sister,   25
And each unto other mindful of favors.

> Beowulf gives Hygd the necklace that Wealhtheow had given
> him.

I am told that to Hygd he proffered the necklace,
Wonder-gem rare that Wealhtheow gave him,
The troop-leader's daughter, a trio of horses
Slender and saddle-bright; soon did the jewel   30
Embellish her bosom, when the beer-feast was over.
So Ecgtheow's bairn brave did prove him,

> Beowulf is famous.

War-famous man, by deeds that were valiant,
He lived in honor, belovèd companions
Slew not carousing; his mood was not cruel,   35
But by hand-strength hugest of heroes then living
The brave one retained the bountiful gift that
The Lord had allowed him. Long was he wretched,
So that sons of the Geatmen accounted him worthless,
And the lord of the liegemen loth was to do him   40

---

of his favor, kindness' sounds well; but 'his' is badly placed to limit 'ést.'—
Perhaps, 'eft' with verbs of saying may have the force of Lat. prefix 're,'
and the H.-So. reading mean, 'that I should its origin rehearse to thee.'

Mickle of honor, when mead-cups were passing;
They fully believed him idle and sluggish,

> He is requited for the slights suffered in earlier days.

An indolent atheling: to the honor-blest man there
Came requital for the cuts he had suffered.
The folk-troop's defender bade fetch to the building   45
The heirloom of Hrethel, embellished with gold,

> Higelac overwhelms the conqueror with gifts.

So the brave one enjoined it; there was jewel no richer
In the form of a weapon 'mong Geats of that era;
In Beowulf's keeping he placed it and gave him
Seven of thousands, manor and lordship.   50
Common to both was land 'mong the people,
Estate and inherited rights and possessions,
To the second one specially spacious dominions,
To the one who was better. It afterward happened
In days that followed, befell the battle-thanes,   55

> After Heardred's death, Beowulf becomes king.

After Higelac's death, and when Heardred was
    murdered
With weapons of warfare 'neath well-covered targets,
When valiant battlemen in victor-band sought him,
War-Scylfing heroes harassed the nephew
Of Hereric in battle. To Beowulf's keeping   60
Turned there in time extensive dominions:

> He rules the Geats fifty years.

He fittingly ruled them a fifty of winters
(He a man-ruler wise was, manor-ward old) till
A certain one 'gan, on gloom-darkening nights, a

> The fire-drake.

Dragon, to govern, who guarded a treasure,   65
A high-rising stone-cliff, on heath that was grayish:
A path 'neath it lay, unknown unto mortals.

Some one of earthmen entered the mountain,
The heathenish hoard laid hold of with ardor;

* * * * * * *   70
* * * * * * *
* * * * * * *
* * * * * * *
* * * * * * *

XXXII.

The Hoard and the Dragon

* * * * * * *

He sought of himself who sorely did harm him,
But, for need very pressing, the servant of one of
The sons of the heroes hate-blows evaded,
Seeking for shelter and the sin-driven warrior   5
Took refuge within there. He early looked in it,
* * * * * * *

* * * * * * *

* * * * * when the onset surprised him,
    The hoard.
He a gem-vessel saw there: many of suchlike   10
Ancient ornaments in the earth-cave were lying,
As in days of yore some one of men of
Illustrious lineage, as a legacy monstrous,
There had secreted them, careful and thoughtful,
Dear-valued jewels. Death had offsnatched them,   15
In the days of the past, and the one man moreover
Of the flower of the folk who fared there the longest,
Was fain to defer it, friend-mourning warder,
A little longer to be left in enjoyment

Of long-lasting treasure.[1] A barrow all-ready   20
Stood on the plain the stream-currents nigh to,
New by the ness-edge, unnethe of approaching:
The keeper of rings carried within a
[2]Ponderous deal of the treasure of nobles,
Of gold that was beaten, briefly he spake then:[3]   25

       The ring-giver bewails the loss of retainers.

'Hold thou, O Earth, now heroes no more may,
The earnings of earlmen. Lo! erst in thy bosom
Worthy men won them; war-death hath ravished,
Perilous life-bale, all my warriors,
Liegemen belovèd, who this life have forsaken,   30
Who hall-pleasures saw. No sword-bearer have I,
And no one to burnish the gold-plated vessel,
The high-valued beaker: my heroes are vanished.
The hardy helmet behung with gilding
Shall be reaved of its riches: the ring-cleansers slumber 35
Who were charged to have ready visors-for-battle,
And the burnie that bided in battle-encounter
O'er breaking of war-shields the bite of the edges
Moulds with the hero. The ring-twisted armor,
Its lord being lifeless, no longer may journey   40
Hanging by heroes; harp-joy is vanished,
The rapture of glee-wood, no excellent falcon
Swoops through the building, no swift-footed charger
Grindeth the gravel. A grievous destruction
No few of the world-folk widely hath scattered!'   45
So, woful of spirit one after all

---

[1] For 'long-gestréona,' B. suggests 'láengestréona,' and renders, *Of fleeting treasures*. S. accepts H.'s 'long-gestréona,' but renders, *The treasure long in accumulating*.

[2] For 'hard-fyrdne' (2246), B. first suggested 'hard-fyndne,' rendering: *A heap of treasures . . . so great that its equal would be hard to find*. The same scholar suggests later 'hord-wynne dæl' = *A deal of treasure-joy*.

[3] Some read 'fec-word' (2247), and render: *Banning words uttered*.

Lamented mournfully, moaning in sadness
By day and by night, till death with its billows
> The fire-dragon

Dashed on his spirit. Then the ancient dusk-scather
Found the great treasure standing all open,   50
He who flaming and fiery flies to the barrows,
Naked war-dragon, nightly escapeth
Encompassed with fire; men under heaven
Widely beheld him. 'Tis said that he looks for[4]
The hoard in the earth, where old he is guarding   55
The heathenish treasure; he'll be nowise the better.
> The dragon meets his match.

So three-hundred winters the waster of peoples
Held upon earth that excellent hoard-hall,
Till the forementioned earlman angered him bitterly:
The beat-plated beaker he bare to his chieftain   60
And fullest remission for all his remissness
Begged of his liegelord. Then the hoard[5] was discovered,
The treasure was taken, his petition was granted
> The hero plunders the dragon's den

The lorn-mooded liegeman. His lord regarded
The old-work of earth-folk—'twas the earliest occasion.   65
When the dragon awoke, the strife was renewed there;
He snuffed 'long the stone then, stout-hearted found he
The footprint of foeman; too far had he gone
With cunning craftiness close to the head of
The fire-spewing dragon. So undoomed he may 'scape
from   70
Anguish and exile with ease who possesseth

---

[4] An earlier reading of H.'s gave the following meaning to this passage: *He is said to inhabit a mound under the earth, where he, etc.* The translation in the text is more authentic.

[5] The repetition of 'hord' in this passage has led some scholars to suggest new readings to avoid the second 'hord.' This, however, is not under the main stress, and, it seems to me, might easily be accepted.

The favor of Heaven. The hoard-warden eagerly
Searched o'er the ground then, would meet with the person
That caused him sorrow while in slumber reclining:
Gleaming and wild he oft went round the cavern,   75
All of it outward; not any of earthmen
Was seen in that desert.[6] Yet he joyed in the battle,
Rejoiced in the conflict: oft he turned to the barrow,
Sought for the gem-cup;[7] this he soon perceived then

> The dragon perceives that some one has disturbed his
> treasure.

That some man or other had discovered the gold,   80
The famous folk-treasure. Not fain did the hoard-ward
Wait until evening; then the ward of the barrow
Was angry in spirit, the loathèd one wished to
Pay for the dear-valued drink-cup with fire.
Then the day was done as the dragon would have it,   85
He no longer would wait on the wall, but departed

> The dragon is infuriated.

Fire-impelled, flaming. Fearful the start was
To earls in the land, as it early thereafter
To their giver-of-gold was grievously ended.

[6] The reading of H.-So. is well defended in the notes to that volume. B. emends and renders: *Nor was there any man in that desert who rejoiced in conflict, in battle-work.* That is, the hoard-ward could not find any one who had disturbed his slumbers, for no warrior was there, t.B.'s emendation would give substantially the same translation.

[7] 'Sinc-fæt' (2301): this word both here and in v. 2232, t.B. renders 'treasure.'

XXXIII.

Brave Though Aged—Reminiscences

The dragon spits fire.

The stranger began then to vomit forth fire,
To burn the great manor; the blaze then glimmered
For anguish to earlmen, not anything living
Was the hateful air-goer willing to leave there.
The war of the worm widely was noticed,   5
The feud of the foeman afar and anear,
How the enemy injured the earls of the Geatmen,
Harried with hatred: back he hied to the treasure,
To the well-hidden cavern crc thc coming of daylight.
He had circled with fire the folk of those regions,   10
With brand and burning; in the barrow he trusted,
In the wall and his war-might: the weening deceived him.

Beowulf hears of the havoc wrought by the dragon.

Then straight was the horror to Beowulf published,
Early forsooth, that his own native homestead,[1]
The best of buildings, was burning and melting,   15
Gift-seat of Geatmen. 'Twas a grief to the spirit
Of the good-mooded hero, the greatest of sorrows:

He fears that Heaven is punishing him for some crime.

---

[1] 'Hám' (2326), the suggestion of B. is accepted by t.B. and other scholars.

The wise one weened then that wielding his kingdom
'Gainst the ancient commandments, he had bitterly angered
The Lord everlasting: with lorn meditations   20
His bosom welled inward, as was nowise his custom.
The fire-spewing dragon fully had wasted
The fastness of warriors, the water-land outward,
The manor with fire. The folk-ruling hero,
Prince of the Weders, was planning to wreak him.   25
The warmen's defender bade them to make him,
Earlmen's atheling, an excellent war-shield

    He orders an iron shield to be made for him, wood is useless.

Wholly of iron: fully he knew then
That wood from the forest was helpless to aid him,
Shield against fire. The long-worthy ruler   30
Must live the last of his limited earth-days,
Of life in the world and the worm along with him,
Though he long had been holding hoard-wealth in plenty.

    He determines to fight alone.

Then the ring-prince disdained to seek with a war-band,
With army extensive, the air-going ranger;   35
He felt no fear of the foeman's assaults and
He counted for little the might of the dragon,
His power and prowess: for previously dared he

    Beowulf's early triumphs referred to

A heap of hostility, hazarded dangers,
War-thane, when Hrothgar's palace he cleansèd,   40
Conquering combatant, clutched in the battle
The kinsmen of Grendel, of kindred detested.[2]

    Higelac's death recalled.

'Twas of hand-fights not least where Higelac was slaughtered,
When the king of the Geatmen with clashings of battle,

---

[2] For 'láðan cynnes' (2355), t.B. suggests 'láðan cynne,' apposition to
'mægum.' From syntactical and other considerations, this is a most excellent
emendation.

Friend-lord of folks in Frisian dominions,   45
Offspring of Hrethrel perished through sword-drink,
With battle-swords beaten; thence Beowulf came then
On self-help relying, swam through the waters;
He bare on his arm, lone-going, thirty
Outfits of armor, when the ocean he mounted.   50
The Hetwars by no means had need to be boastful
Of their fighting afoot, who forward to meet him
Carried their war-shields: not many returned from
The brave-mooded battle-knight back to their homesteads.
Ecgtheow's bairn o'er the bight-courses swam then,   55
Lone-goer lorn to his land-folk returning,
Where Hygd to him tendered treasure and kingdom,
> Heardred's lack of capacity to rule.
Rings and dominion: her son she not trusted,
To be able to keep the kingdom devised him
'Gainst alien races, on the death of King Higelac.   60
> Beowulf's tact and delicacy recalled.
Yet the sad ones succeeded not in persuading the atheling
In any way ever, to act as a suzerain
To Heardred, or promise to govern the kingdom;
Yet with friendly counsel in the folk he sustained him,
Gracious, with honor, till he grew to be older,   65
> Reference is here made to a visit which Beowulf receives
> from Eanmund and Eadgils, why they come is not known.
Wielded the Weders. Wide-fleeing outlaws,
Ohthere's sons, sought him o'er the waters:
They had stirred a revolt 'gainst the helm of the Scylfings,
The best of the sea-kings, who in Swedish dominions
Distributed treasure, distinguished folk-leader.   70
'Twas the end of his earth-days; injury fatal[3]
By swing of the sword he received as a greeting,

---

[3] Gr. read 'on feorme' (2386), rendering: *He there at the banquet a fatal wound received by blows of the sword.*

Offspring of Higelac; Ongentheow's bairn
Later departed to visit his homestead,
When Heardred was dead; let Beowulf rule them,   75
Govern the Geatmen: good was that folk-king.

XXXIV.

Beowulf Seeks the Dragon—Beowulf's Reminiscences

He planned requital for the folk-leader's ruin
In days thereafter, to Eadgils the wretched
Becoming an enemy. Ohthere's son then
Went with a war-troop o'er the wide-stretching currents
With warriors and weapons: with woe-journeys cold he   5
After avenged him, the king's life he took.

     Beowulf has been preserved through many perils.

So he came off uninjured from all of his battles,
Perilous fights, offspring of Ecgtheow,
From his deeds of daring, till that day most momentous
When he fate-driven fared to fight with the dragon.   10

     With eleven comrades, he seeks the dragon.

With eleven companions the prince of the Geatmen
Went lowering with fury to look at the fire-drake:
Inquiring he'd found how the feud had arisen,
Hate to his heroes; the highly-famed gem-vessel
Was brought to his keeping through the hand of th'
    informer.   15

     A guide leads the way, but

That in the throng was thirteenth of heroes,
That caused the beginning of conflict so bitter,

Captive and wretched, must sad-mooded thenceward
　　very reluctantly.
Point out the place: he passed then unwillingly
To the spot where he knew of the notable cavern,　　20
The cave under earth, not far from the ocean,
The anger of eddies, which inward was full of
Jewels and wires: a warden uncanny,
Warrior weaponed, wardered the treasure,
Old under earth; no easy possession　　25
For any of earth-folk access to get to.
Then the battle-brave atheling sat on the naze-edge,
While the gold-friend of Geatmen gracious saluted
His fireside-companions: woe was his spirit,
Death-boding, wav'ring; Weird very near him,　　30
Who must seize the old hero, his soul-treasure look for,
Dragging aloof his life from his body:
Not flesh-hidden long was the folk-leader's spirit.
Beowulf spake, Ecgtheow's son:
　　Beowulf's retrospect.
'I survived in my youth-days many a conflict,　　35
Hours of onset: that all I remember.
I was seven-winters old when the jewel-prince took me,
High-lord of heroes, at the hands of my father,
Hrethel the hero-king had me in keeping,
　　Hrethel took me when I was seven.
Gave me treasure and feasting, our kinship
　　remembered;　　40
Not ever was I *any* less dear to him
　　He treated me as a son.
Knight in the boroughs, than the bairns of his household,
Herebald and Hæthcyn and Higelac mine.
To the eldest unjustly by acts of a kinsman
Was murder-bed strewn, since him Hæthcyn from
　　horn-bow　　45
　　One of the brothers accidentally kills another.

His sheltering chieftain shot with an arrow,
Erred in his aim and injured his kinsman,
One brother the other, with blood-sprinkled spear:
> No fee could compound for such a calamity.
'Twas a feeless fight, finished in malice,
Sad to his spirit; the folk-prince however   50
Had to part from existence with vengeance untaken.
> [A parallel case is supposed.]
So to hoar-headed hero 'tis heavily crushing[1]
To live to see his son as he rideth
Young on the gallows: then measures he chanteth,
A song of sorrow, when his son is hanging   55
For the raven's delight, and aged and hoary
He is unable to offer any assistance.
Every morning his offspring's departure
Is constant recalled: he cares not to wait for
The birth of an heir in his borough-enclosures,   60
Since that one through death-pain the deeds hath
> experienced.
He heart-grieved beholds in the house of his son the

---

[1] 'Gomelum ceorle' (2445).—H. takes these words as referring to Hrethel;
but the translator here departs from his editor by understanding the poet
to refer to a hypothetical old man, introduced as an illustration of a father's
sorrow.

Hrethrel had certainly never seen a son of his ride on the gallows to feed
the crows.

The passage beginning 'swá bið géomorlic' seems to be an effort to reach
a full simile, 'as . . . so.' 'As it is mournful for an old man, etc. . . . so the
defence of the Weders (2463) bore heart-sorrow, etc.' The verses 2451 to
2463 would be parenthetical, the poet's feelings being so strong as to
interrupt the simile. The punctuation of the fourth edition would be
better—a comma after 'galgan' (2447). The translation may be indicated
as follows: *(Just) as it is sad for an old man to see his son ride young on the
gallows when he himself is uttering mournful measures, a sorrowful song,
while his son hangs for a comfort to the raven, and he, old and infirm, cannot
render him any help—(he is constantly reminded, etc., 2451–2463)—so the
defence of the Weders, etc.*

Wine-building wasted, the wind-lodging places
Reaved of their roaring; the riders are sleeping,
The knights in the grave; there's no sound of the
      harp-wood,   65
Joy in the yards, as of yore were familiar.

XXXV.

Reminiscences (*Continued*)—Beowulf's Last Battle

'He seeks then his chamber, singeth a woe-song
One for the other; all too extensive
Seemed homesteads and plains. So the helm of the Weders
      Hrethel grieves for Herebald.
Mindful of Herebald heart-sorrow carried,
Stirred with emotion, nowise was able   5
To wreak his ruin on the ruthless destroyer:
He was unable to follow the warrior with hatred,
With deeds that were direful, though dear he not held him.
Then pressed by the pang this pain occasioned him,
He gave up glee, God-light elected;   10
He left to his sons, as the man that is rich does,
His land and fortress, when from life he departed.
      Strife between Swedes and Geats.
Then was crime and hostility 'twixt Swedes and Geatmen,
O'er wide-stretching water warring was mutual,
Burdensome hatred, when Hrethel had perished,   15
And Ongentheow's offspring were active and valiant,
Wished not to hold to peace oversea, but
Round Hreosna-beorh often accomplished
Cruelest massacre. This my kinsman avengèd,

The feud and fury, as 'tis found on inquiry,   20
Though one of them paid it with forfeit of life-joys,
     Hæthcyn's fall at Ravenswood.
With price that was hard: the struggle became then
Fatal to Hæthcyn, lord of the Geatmen.
Then I heard that at morning one brother the other
With edges of irons egged on to murder,   25
Where Ongentheow maketh onset on Eofor:
The helmet crashed, the hoary-haired Scylfing
Sword-smitten fell, his hand then remembered
Feud-hate sufficient, refused not the death-blow.
     I requited him for the jewels he gave me.
The gems that he gave me, with jewel-bright sword I   30
'Quited in contest, as occasion was offered:
Land he allowed me, life-joy at homestead,
Manor to live on. Little he needed
From Gepids or Danes or in Sweden to look for
Trooper less true, with treasure to buy him;   35
'Mong foot-soldiers ever in front I would hie me,
Alone in the vanguard, and evermore gladly
Warfare shall wage, while this weapon endureth
That late and early often did serve me
     Beowulf refers to his having slain Dæghrefn.
When I proved before heroes the slayer of Dæghrefn,   40
Knight of the Hugmen: he by no means was suffered
To the king of the Frisians to carry the jewels,
The breast-decoration; but the banner-possessor
Bowed in the battle, brave-mooded atheling.
No weapon was slayer, but war-grapple broke then   45
The surge of his spirit, his body destroying.
Now shall weapon's edge make war for the treasure,
And hand and firm-sword.' Beowulf spake then,
Boast-words uttered—the latest occasion:
     He boasts of his youthful prowess, and declares himself still
     fearless.

'I braved in my youth-days battles unnumbered;   50
Still am I willing the struggle to look for,
Fame-deeds perform, folk-warden prudent,
If the hateful despoiler forth from his cavern
Seeketh me out!' Each of the heroes,
Helm-bearers sturdy, he thereupon greeted   55

> His last salutations.

Belovèd co-liegemen—his last salutation:
'No brand would I bear, no blade for the dragon,
Wist I a way my word-boast to 'complish[1]
Else with the monster, as with Grendel I did it;
But fire in the battle hot I expect there,   60
Furious flame-burning: so I fixed on my body
Target and war-mail. The ward of the barrow[2]
I'll not flee from a foot-length, the foeman uncanny.
At the wall 'twill befall us as Fate decreeth,

> Let Fate decide between us.

Each one's Creator. I am eager in spirit,   65
With the wingèd war-hero to away with all boasting.
Bide on the barrow with burnies protected,

> Wait ye here till the battle is over.

Earls in armor, which of *us* two may better
Bear his disaster, when the battle is over.
'Tis no matter of yours, and man cannot do it,   70
But me and me only, to measure his strength with
The monster of malice, might-deeds to 'complish.
I with prowess shall gain the gold, or the battle,
Direful death-woe will drag off your ruler!'

---

[1] The clause 2520(2)–2522(1), rendered by 'Wist I . . . monster,' Gr.,
followed by S., translates substantially as follows: *If I knew how else I might
combat the boastful defiance of the monster.*—The translation turns upon
'wiðgrípan,' a word not understood.

[2] B. emends and translates: *I will not flee the space of a foot from the guard
of the barrow, but there shall be to us a fight at the wall, as fate decrees, each
one's Creator.*

The mighty champion rose by his shield then,   75
Brave under helmet, in battle-mail went he
'Neath steep-rising stone-cliffs, the strength he relied on
Of one man alone: no work for a coward.
Then he saw by the wall who a great many battles
Had lived through, most worthy, when foot-troops
    collided,   80

    The place of strife is described.

Stone-arches standing, stout-hearted champion,
Saw a brook from the barrow bubbling out thenceward:
The flood of the fountain was fuming with war-flame:
Not nigh to the hoard, for season the briefest
Could he brave, without burning, the abyss that was
    yawning,   85
The drake was so fiery. The prince of the Weders
Caused then that words came from his bosom,
So fierce was his fury; the firm-hearted shouted:
His battle-clear voice came in resounding
'Neath the gray-colored stone. Stirred was his hatred,   90

    Beowulf calls out under the stone arches.

The hoard-ward distinguished the speech of a man;
Time was no longer to look out for friendship.
The breath of the monster issued forth first,
Vapory war-sweat, out of the stone-cave:

    The terrible encounter.

The earth re-echoed. The earl 'neath the barrow   95
Lifted his shield, lord of the Geatmen,
Tow'rd the terrible stranger: the ring-twisted creature's
Heart was then ready to seek for a struggle.

    Beowulf brandishes his sword,

The excellent battle-king first brandished his weapon,
The ancient heirloom, of edges unblunted,[3]   100

---

[3] The translation of this passage is based on 'unsláw' (2565), accepted by
H.-So., in lieu of the long-standing 'ungléaw.' The former is taken as an

128

To the death-planners twain was terror from other.

> and stands against his shield.

The lord of the troopers intrepidly stood then
'Gainst his high-rising shield, when the dragon coiled him

> The dragon coils himself.

Quickly together: in corslet he bided.
He went then in blazes, bended and striding,   105
Hasting him forward. His life and body
The targe well protected, for time-period shorter
Than wish demanded for the well-renowned leader,
Where he then for the first day was forced to be victor,
Famous in battle, as Fate had not willed it.   110
The lord of the Geatmen uplifted his hand then,
Smiting the fire-drake with sword that was precious,
That bright on the bone the blade-edge did weaken,
Bit more feebly than his folk-leader needed,
Burdened with bale-griefs. Then the barrow-protector,   115

> The dragon rages.

When the sword-blow had fallen, was fierce in his spirit,
Flinging his fires, flamings of battle
Gleamed then afar: the gold-friend of Weders

> Beowulf's sword fails him.

Boasted no conquests, his battle-sword failed him
Naked in conflict, as by no means it ought to,   120
Long-trusty weapon. 'Twas no slight undertaking
That Ecgtheow's famous offspring would leave
The drake-cavern's bottom; he must live in some region
Other than this, by the will of the dragon,
As each one of earthmen existence must forfeit.   125
'Twas early thereafter the excellent warriors

> The combat is renewed.

---

adj. limiting 'sweord'; the latter as an adj. c. 'gúð-cyning': *The good war-king, rash with edges, brandished his sword, his old relic.* The latter gives a more rhetorical Anglo-Saxon (poetical) sentence.

Met with each other. Anew and afresh
The hoard-ward took heart (gasps heaved then his bosom):
    The great hero is reduced to extremities.
Sorrow he suffered encircled with fire
Who the people erst governed. His companions by no
    means   130
Were banded about him, bairns of the princes,
    His comrades flee!
With valorous spirit, but they sped to the forest,
Seeking for safety. The soul-deeps of one were
    Blood is thicker than water.
Ruffled by care: kin-love can never
Aught in him waver who well doth consider.   135

XXXVI.

Wiglaf the Trusty—Beowulf is Deserted
by Friends and by Sword

Wiglaf remains true—the ideal Teutonic liegeman.

The son of Weohstan was Wiglaf entitled,
Shield-warrior precious, prince of the Scylfings,
Ælfhere's kinsman: he saw his dear liegelord
Enduring the heat 'neath helmet and visor.
Then he minded the holding that erst he had given him, 5

Wiglaf recalls Beowulf's generosity.

The Wægmunding warriors' wealth-blessèd homestead,
Each of the folk-rights his father had wielded;
He was hot for the battle, his hand seized the target,
The yellow-bark shield, he unsheathed his old weapon,
Which was known among earthmen as the relic of
    Eanmund,   10
Ohthere's offspring, whom, exiled and friendless,
Weohstan did slay with sword-edge in battle,
And carried his kinsman the clear-shining helmet,
The ring-made burnie, the old giant-weapon
That Onela gave him, his boon-fellow's armor,   15
Ready war-trappings: he the feud did not mention,
Though he'd fatally smitten the son of his brother.
Many a half-year held he the treasures,

The bill and the burnie, till his bairn became able,
Like his father before him, fame-deeds to 'complish; 20
Then he gave him 'mong Geatmen a goodly array of
Weeds for his warfare; he went from life then
Old on his journey. 'Twas the earliest time then

> This is Wiglaf's first battle as liegeman of Beowulf.

That the youthful champion might charge in the battle
Aiding his liegelord; his spirit was dauntless. 25
Nor did kinsman's bequest quail at the battle:
This the dragon discovered on their coming together.
Wiglaf uttered many a right-saying,
Said to his fellows, sad was his spirit:

> Wiglaf appeals to the pride of the cowards.

'I remember the time when, tasting the mead-cup, 30
We promised in the hall the lord of us all
Who gave us these ring-treasures, that this battle-equipment,
Swords and helmets, we'd certainly quite him,
Should need of such aid ever befall him:

> How we have forfeited our liegelord's confidence! 35

In the war-band he chose us for this journey
    spontaneously, 35
Stirred us to glory and gave me these jewels,
Since he held and esteemed us trust-worthy spearmen,
Hardy helm-bearers, though this hero-achievement
Our lord intended alone to accomplish,
Ward of his people, for most of achievements, 40
Doings audacious, he did among earth-folk.

> Our lord is in sore need of us.

The day is now come when the ruler of earthmen
Needeth the vigor of valiant heroes:
Let us wend us towards him, the war-prince to succor,
While the heat yet rageth, horrible fire-fight. 45

> I would rather die than go home with out my suzerain.

God wot in me, 'tis mickle the liefer

The blaze should embrace my body and eat it
With my treasure-bestower. Meseemeth not proper
To bear our battle-shields back to our country,
'Less first we are able to fell and destroy the   50
Long-hating foeman, to defend the life of

> Surely he does not deserve to die alone.

The prince of the Weders. Well do I know 'tisn't
Earned by his exploits, he only of Geatmen
Sorrow should suffer, sink in the battle:
Brand and helmet to us both shall be common,   55
[1]Shield-cover, burnie.' Through the bale-smoke he stalked
    then,
Went under helmet to the help of his chieftain,

> Wiglaf reminds Beowulf of his youthful boasts.

Briefly discoursing: 'Beowulf dear,
Perform thou all fully, as thou formerly saidst,
In thy youthful years, that while yet thou livedst   60
Thou wouldst let thine honor not ever be lessened.
Thy life thou shalt save, mighty in actions,
Atheling undaunted, with all of thy vigor;

> The monster advances on them.

I'll give thee assistance.' The dragon came raging,
Wild-mooded stranger, when these words had been
    uttered   65
('Twas the second occasion), seeking his enemies,
Men that were hated, with hot-gleaming fire-waves;
With blaze-billows burned the board to its edges:
The fight-armor failed then to furnish assistance

---

[1] The passage 'Brand . . . burnie,' is much disputed. In the first place, some eminent critics assume a gap of at least two half-verses.—'Úrum' (2660), being a peculiar form, has been much discussed. 'Byrdu-scrúd' is also a crux. B. suggests 'býwdu-scrúd' = *splendid vestments*. Nor is 'bám' accepted by all, 'béon' being suggested. Whatever the individual words, the passage must mean, '*I intend to share with him my equipments of defence*.'

To the youthful spear-hero: but the young-agèd
    stripling   70
Quickly advanced 'neath his kinsman's war-target,
Since his own had been ground in the grip of the fire.

    Beowulf strikes at the dragon.

Then the warrior-king was careful of glory,
He soundly smote with sword-for-the-battle,
That it stood in the head by hatred driven;   75
Nægling was shivered, the old and iron-made

      His sword fails him.

Brand of Beowulf in battle deceived him.
'Twas denied him that edges of irons were able
To help in the battle; the hand was too mighty
[2]Which every weapon, as I heard on inquiry,   80
Outstruck in its stroke, when to struggle he carried
The wonderful war-sword: it waxed him no better.

    The dragon advances on Beowulf again.

Then the people-despoiler—third of his onsets—
Fierce-raging fire-drake, of feud-hate was mindful,
Charged on the strong one, when chance was afforded, 85
Heated and war-grim, seized on his neck
With teeth that were bitter; he bloody did wax with
Soul-gore seething; sword-blood in waves boiled.

---

[2] B. would render: *Which, as I heard, excelled in stroke every sword that
he carried to the strife, even the strongest (sword).* For 'Þonne' he reads
'Þone,' rel. pr.

XXXVII.

The Fatal Struggle—Beowulf's Last Moments

Wiglaf defends Beowulf.

Then I heard that at need of the king of the people
The upstanding earlman exhibited prowess,
Vigor and courage, as suited his nature;
[1]He his head did not guard, but the high-minded liegeman's
Hand was consumed, when he succored his kinsman,   5
So he struck the strife-bringing strange-comer lower,
Earl-thane in armor, that *in* went the weapon
Gleaming and plated, that 'gan then the fire[2]

Beowulf draws his knife,

Later to lessen. The liegelord himself then
Retained his consciousness, brandished his war-knife,   10
Battle-sharp, bitter, that he bare on his armor:

and cuts the dragon.

---

[1] B. renders: *He* (W.) *did not regard his* (the dragon's) *head* (since Beowulf had struck it without effect), *but struck the dragon a little lower down.*—One crux is to find out *whose head* is meant; another is to bring out the antithesis between 'head' and 'hand.'

[2] 'Þæt þæt fýr' (2702), S. emends to 'þá þæt fýr' = *when the fire began to grow less intense afterward*. This emendation relieves the passage of a plethora of conjunctive *þæt*'s.

The Weder-lord cut the worm in the middle.
They had felled the enemy (life drove out then[3]
Puissant prowess), the pair had destroyed him,
Land-chiefs related: so a liegeman should prove him,   15
A thaneman when needed. To the prince 'twas the last of
His era of conquest by his own great achievements,

     Beowulf's wound swells and burns.

The latest of world-deeds. The wound then began
Which the earth-dwelling dragon erstwhile had wrought him
To burn and to swell. He soon then discovered   20
That bitterest bale-woe in his bosom was raging,
Poison within. The atheling advanced then,

     He sits down exhausted.

That along by the wall, he prudent of spirit
Might sit on a settle; he saw the giant-work,
How arches of stone strengthened with pillars   25
The earth-hall eternal inward supported.
Then the long-worthy liegeman laved with his hand the

     Wiglaf bathes his lord's head.

Far-famous chieftain, gory from sword-edge,
Refreshing the face of his friend-lord and ruler,
Sated with battle, unbinding his helmet.   30
Beowulf answered, of his injury spake he,
His wound that was fatal (he was fully aware
He had lived his allotted life-days enjoying
The pleasures of earth; then past was entirely
His measure of days, death very near):   35

---

[3] For 'gefyldan' (2707), S. proposes 'gefylde.' The passage would read: *He
felled the foe (life drove out strength), and they then both had destroyed him,
chieftains related.* This gives Beowulf the credit of having felled the dragon;
then they combine to annihilate him.—For 'ellen' (2707), Kl. suggests 'e(a)
llne.'—The reading '*life drove out strength*' is very unsatisfactory and very
peculiar. I would suggest as follows: Adopt S.'s emendation, remove H.'s
parenthesis, read 'ferh-ellen wræc,' and translate: *He felled the foe, drove
out his life-strength* (that is, made him *hors de combat*), *and then they both,*
etc.

Beowulf regrets that he has no son.

'My son I would give now my battle-equipments,
Had any of heirs been after me granted,
Along of my body. This people I governed
Fifty of winters: no king 'mong my neighbors
Dared to encounter me with comrades-in-battle,   40
Try me with terror. The time to me ordered
I bided at home, mine own kept fitly,
Sought me no snares, swore me not many

I can rejoice in a well-spent life.

Oaths in injustice. Joy over all this
I'm able to have, though ill with my death-wounds;   45
Hence the Ruler of Earthmen need not charge me
With the killing of kinsmen, when cometh my life out
Forth from my body. Fare thou with haste now

Bring me the hoard, Wiglaf, that my dying eyes may be
refreshed by a sight of it.

To behold the hoard 'neath the hoar-grayish stone,
Well-lovèd Wiglaf, now the worm is a-lying,   50
Sore-wounded sleepeth, disseized of his treasure.
Go thou in haste that treasures of old I,
Gold-wealth may gaze on, together see lying
The ether-bright jewels, be easier able,
Having the heap of hoard-gems, to yield my   55
Life and the land-folk whom long I have governed.'

XXXVIII.

Wiglaf Plunders the Dragon's Den—Beowulf's Death

Wiglaf fulfils his lord's behest.

Then heard I that Wihstan's son very quickly,
These words being uttered, heeded his liegelord
Wounded and war-sick, went in his armor,
His well-woven ring-mail, 'neath the roof of the barrow.
Then the trusty retainer treasure-gems many   5

The dragon's den.

Victorious saw, when the seat he came near to,
Gold-treasure sparkling spread on the bottom,
Wonder on the wall, and the worm-creature's cavern,
The ancient dawn-flier's, vessels a-standing,
Cups of the ancients of cleansers bereavèd,   10
Robbed of their ornaments: there were helmets in numbers,
Old and rust-eaten, arm-bracelets many,
Artfully woven. Wealth can easily,
Gold on the sea-bottom, turn into vanity[1]

---

[1] The word 'oferhígian' (2767) being vague and little understood, two quite distinct translations of this passage have arisen. One takes 'oferhígian' as meaning 'to exceed,' and, inserting 'hord' after 'gehwone,' renders: *The treasure may easily, the gold in the ground, exceed in value every hoard of man, hide it who will.* The other takes 'oferhígian' as meaning 'to render

Each one of earthmen, arm him who pleaseth! 15
And he saw there lying an all-golden banner
High o'er the hoard, of hand-wonders greatest,
Linkèd with lacets: a light from it sparkled,
That the floor of the cavern he was able to look on,

    The dragon is not there.

To examine the jewels. Sight of the dragon 20
Not any was offered, but edge offcarried him.

    Wiglaf bears the hoard away.

Then I heard that the hero the hoard-treasure plundered,
The giant-work ancient reaved in the cavern,
Bare on his bosom the beakers and platters,
As himself would fain have it, and took off the
    standard, 25
The brightest of beacons;[2] the bill had erst injured
(Its edge was of iron), the old-ruler's weapon,
Him who long had watched as ward of the jewels,
Who fire-terror carried hot for the treasure,
Rolling in battle, in middlemost darkness, 30
Till murdered he perished. The messenger hastened,
Not loth to return, hurried by jewels:
Curiosity urged him if, excellent-mooded,
Alive he should find the lord of the Weders
Mortally wounded, at the place where he left him. 35
'Mid the jewels he found then the famous old chieftain,
His liegelord belovèd, at his life's-end gory:
He thereupon 'gan to lave him with water,
Till the point of his word piercèd his breast-hoard.

---

arrogant,' and, giving the sentence a moralizing tone, renders substantially
as in the body of this work. (Cf. **28** 13 et seq.)

[2] The passage beginning here is very much disputed. 'The bill of the old
lord' is by some regarded as Beowulf's sword; by others, as that of the
ancient possessor of the hoard. 'Ǣr gescód' (2778), translated in this work
as verb and adverb, is by some regarded as a compound participial adj.
= *sheathed in brass.*

Beowulf spake (the gold-gems he noticed),   40

    Beowulf is rejoiced to see the jewels.

The old one in sorrow: 'For the jewels I look on
Thanks do I utter for all to the Ruler,
Wielder of Worship, with words of devotion,
The Lord everlasting, that He let me such treasures
Gain for my people ere death overtook me.   45
Since I've bartered the agèd life to me granted
For treasure of jewels, attend ye henceforward

    He desires to be held in memory by his people.

The wants of the war-thanes; I can wait here no longer.
The battle-famed bid ye to build them a grave-hill,
Bright when I'm burned, at the brim-current's limit;   50
As a memory-mark to the men I have governed,
Aloft it shall tower on Whale's-Ness uprising,
That earls of the ocean hereafter may call it
Beowulf's barrow, those who barks ever-dashing
From a distance shall drive o'er the darkness of waters.' 55

    The hero's last gift

The bold-mooded troop-lord took from his neck then
The ring that was golden, gave to his liegeman,
The youthful war-hero, his gold-flashing helmet,
His collar and war-mail, bade him well to enjoy them:

    and last words.

'Thou art latest left of the line of our kindred,   60
Of Wægmunding people: Weird hath offcarried
All of my kinsmen to the Creator's glory,
Earls in their vigor: I shall after them fare.'
'Twas the aged liegelord's last-spoken word in
His musings of spirit, ere he mounted the fire,   65
The battle-waves burning: from his bosom departed
His soul to seek the sainted ones' glory.

XXXIX.

The Dead Foes—Wiglaf's Bitter Taunts

Wiglaf is sorely grieved to see his lord look so un-warlike.
It had wofully chanced then the youthful retainer
To behold on earth the most ardent-belovèd
At his life-days' limit, lying there helpless.
The slayer too lay there, of life all bereavèd,
Horrible earth-drake, harassed with sorrow: 5

The dragon has plundered his last hoard.
The round-twisted monster was permitted no longer
To govern the ring-hoards, but edges of war-swords
Mightily seized him, battle-sharp, sturdy
Leavings of hammers, that still from his wounds
The flier-from-farland fell to the earth   10
Hard by his hoard-house, hopped he at midnight
Not e'er through the air, nor exulting in jewels
Suffered them to see him: but he sank then to earthward
Through the hero-chief's handwork. I heard sure it throve
      then

Few warriors dared to face the monster.
But few in the land of liegemen of valor,   15
Though of every achievement bold he had proved him,
To run 'gainst the breath of the venomous scather,
Or the hall of the treasure to trouble with hand-blows,

If he watching had found the ward of the hoard-hall
On the barrow abiding. Beowulf's part of   20
The treasure of jewels was paid for with death;
Each of the twain had attained to the end of
Life so unlasting. Not long was the time till

> The cowardly thanes come out of the thicket.

The tardy-at-battle returned from the thicket,
The timid truce-breakers ten all together,   25
Who durst not before play with the lances
In the prince of the people's pressing emergency;

> They are ashamed of their desertion.

But blushing with shame, with shields they betook them,
With arms and armor where the old one was lying:
They gazed upon Wiglaf. He was sitting exhausted,   30
Foot-going fighter, not far from the shoulders
Of the lord of the people, would rouse him with water;
No whit did it help him; though he hoped for it keenly,
He was able on earth not at all in the leader
Life to retain, and nowise to alter   35
The will of the Wielder; the World-Ruler's power[1]
Would govern the actions of each one of heroes,

> Wiglaf is ready to excoriate them.

As yet He is doing. From the young one forthwith then
Could grim-worded greeting be got for him quickly
Whose courage had failed him. Wiglaf discoursed then,   40
Weohstan his son, sad-mooded hero,

> He begins to taunt them.

Looked on the hated: 'He who soothness will utter
Can say that the liegelord who gave you the jewels,
The ornament-armor wherein ye are standing,
When on ale-bench often he offered to hall-men   45

---

[1] For 'dædum rædan' (2859) B. suggests 'déáð árædan,' and renders: *The
might (or judgment) of God would determine death for every man, as he still
does.*

Helmet and burnie, the prince to his liegemen,
As best upon earth he was able to find him,—
> Surely our lord wasted his armor on poltroons.

That he wildly wasted his war-gear undoubtedly
When battle o'ertook him.[2] The troop-king no need had
To glory in comrades; yet God permitted him,   50
> He, however, got along without you.

Victory-Wielder, with weapon unaided
Himself to avenge, when vigor was needed.
I life-protection but little was able
To give him in battle, and I 'gan, notwithstanding,
> With some aid, I could have saved our liegelord.

Helping my kinsman (my strength overtaxing):   55
He waxed the weaker when with weapon I smote on
My mortal opponent, the fire less strongly
Flamed from his bosom. Too few of protectors
Came round the king at the critical moment.
> Gift-giving is over with your people: the ring-lord is dead.

Now must ornament-taking and weapon-bestowing,   60
Home-joyance all, cease for your kindred,
Food for the people; each of your warriors
Must needs be bereavèd of rights that he holdeth
In landed possessions, when faraway nobles
Shall learn of your leaving your lord so basely,   65
> What is life without honor?

The dastardly deed. Death is more pleasant
To every earlman than infamous life is!'

---

[2] Some critics, H. himself in earlier editions, put the clause, 'When . . . him' (A.-S. 'þá . . . beget') with the following sentence; that is, they make it dependent upon 'þorfte' (2875) instead of upon 'forwurpe' (2873).

XL.

The Messenger of Death

Wiglaf sends the news of Beowulf's death to liegemen near by.

Then he charged that the battle be announced at the hedge
Up o'er the cliff-edge, where the earl-troopers bided
The whole of the morning, mood-wretched sat them,
Bearers of battle-shields, both things expecting,
The end of his lifetime and the coming again of   5
The liegelord belovèd. Little reserved he
Of news that was known, who the ness-cliff did travel,
But he truly discoursed to all that could hear him:

The messenger speaks.

'Now the free-giving friend-lord of the folk of the Weders,
The folk-prince of Geatmen, is fast in his death-bed,   10
By the deeds of the dragon in death-bed abideth;
Along with him lieth his life-taking foeman
Slain with knife-wounds: he was wholly unable
To injure at all the ill-planning monster

Wiglaf sits by our dead lord.

With bite of his sword-edge. Wiglaf is sitting,   15
Offspring of Wihstan, up over Beowulf,
Earl o'er another whose end-day hath reached him,

Head-watch holdeth o'er heroes unliving,[1]

    Our lord's death will lead to attacks from our old foes.

For friend and for foeman. The folk now expecteth
A season of strife when the death of the folk-king   20
To Frankmen and Frisians in far-lands is published.
The war-hatred waxed warm 'gainst the Hugmen,

    Higelac's death recalled.

When Higelac came with an army of vessels
Faring to Friesland, where the Frankmen in battle
Humbled him and bravely with overmight 'complished 25
That the mail-clad warrior must sink in the battle,
Fell 'mid his folk-troop: no fret-gems presented
The atheling to earlmen; aye was denied us
Merewing's mercy. The men of the Swedelands
For truce or for truth trust I but little;   30
But widely 'twas known that near Ravenswood Ongentheow

    Hæthcyn's fall referred to.

Sundered Hæthcyn the Hrethling from life-joys,
When for pride overweening the War-Scylfings first did
Seek the Geatmen with savage intentions.
Early did Ohthere's age-laden father,   35
Old and terrible, give blow in requital,
Killing the sea-king, the queen-mother rescued,
The old one his consort deprived of her gold,
Onela's mother and Ohthere's also,
And then followed the feud-nursing foemen till hardly, 40
Reaved of their ruler, they Ravenswood entered.
Then with vast-numbered forces he assaulted the remnant,
Weary with wounds, woe often promised
The livelong night to the sad-hearted war-troop:

---

[1] 'Hige-méðum' (2910) is glossed by H. as dat. plu. (= for the dead). S. proposes 'hige-méðe,' nom. sing. limiting Wigláf; i.e. *W., mood-weary, holds head-watch o'er friend and foe.*—B. suggests taking the word as dat. inst. plu. of an abstract noun in -'u.' The translation would be substantially the same as S.'s.

Said he at morning would kill them with edges of
    weapons,   45
Some on the gallows for glee to the fowls.
Aid came after to the anxious-in-spirit
At dawn of the day, after Higelac's bugle
And trumpet-sound heard they, when the good one proceeded
And faring followed the flower of the troopers.   50

XLI.

The Messenger's Retrospect

The messenger continues, and refers to the feuds of Swedes
and Geats.

'The blood-stainèd trace of Swedes and Geatmen,
The death-rush of warmen, widely was noticed,
How the folks with each other feud did awaken.
The worthy one went then[1] with well-beloved comrades,
Old and dejected to go to the fastness,   5
Ongentheow earl upward then turned him;
Of Higelac's battle he'd heard on inquiry,
The exultant one's prowess, despaired of resistance,
With earls of the ocean to be able to struggle,
'Gainst sea-going sailors to save the hoard-treasure,   10
His wife and his children; he fled after thenceward
Old 'neath the earth-wall. Then was offered pursuance
To the braves of the Swedemen, the banner[2] to Higelac.

[1] For 'góda,' which seems a surprising epithet for a Geat to apply to the
'terrible' Ongentheow, B. suggests 'gomela.' The passage would then stand:
'*The old one went then,*' etc.

[2] For 'segn Higeláce,' K., Th., and B. propose 'segn Higeláces,' meaning:
Higelac's banner followed the Swedes (in pursuit).—S. suggests 'sæcc
Higeláces,' and renders: *Higelac's pursuit.*—The H.-So. reading, as translated
in our text, means that the banner of the enemy was captured and brought
to Higelac as a trophy.

They fared then forth o'er the field-of-protection,
When the Hrethling heroes hedgeward had thronged
    them.   15
Then with edges of irons was Ongentheow driven,
The gray-haired to tarry, that the troop-ruler had to
Suffer the power solely of Eofor:

    Wulf wounds Ongentheow.

Wulf then wildly with weapon assaulted him,
Wonred his son, that for swinge of the edges   20
The blood from his body burst out in currents,
Forth 'neath his hair. He feared not however,
Gray-headed Scylfing, but speedily quited

    Ongentheow gives a stout blow in return.

The wasting wound-stroke with worse exchange,
When the king of the thane-troop thither did turn him: 25
The wise-mooded son of Wonred was powerless
To give a return-blow to the age-hoary man,
But his head-shielding helmet first hewed he to pieces,
That flecked with gore perforce he did totter,
Fell to the earth; not fey was he yet then,   30
But up did he spring though an edge-wound had reached him.

    Eofor smites Ongentheow fiercely.

Then Higelac's vassal, valiant and dauntless,
When his brother lay dead, made his broad-bladed weapon,
Giant-sword ancient, defence of the giants,
Bound o'er the shield-wall; the folk-prince succumbed
    then,   35

    Ongentheow is slain.

Shepherd of people, was pierced to the vitals.
There were many attendants who bound up his kinsman,
Carried him quickly when occasion was granted
That the place of the slain they were suffered to manage.
This pending, one hero plundered the other,   40
His armor of iron from Ongentheow ravished,
His hard-sword hilted and helmet together;

Eofor takes the old king's war-gear to Higelac.

The old one's equipments he carried to Higelac.
He the jewels received, and rewards 'mid the troopers
Graciously promised, and so did accomplish: 45
The king of the Weders requited the war-rush,
Hrethel's descendant, when home he repaired him,

Higelac rewards the brothers.

To Eofor and Wulf with wide-lavished treasures,
To each of them granted a hundred of thousands
In land and rings wrought out of wire: 50

His gifts were beyond cavil.

None upon mid-earth needed to twit him[3]
With the gifts he gave them, when glory they conquered;

To Eofor he also gives his only daughter in marriage.

And to Eofor then gave he his one only daughter,
The honor of home, as an earnest of favor.
That's the feud and hatred—as ween I 'twill happen—   55
The anger of earthmen, that earls of the Swedemen
Will visit on us, when they hear that our leader
Lifeless is lying, he who longtime protected
His hoard and kingdom 'gainst hating assailers,
Who on the fall of the heroes defended of yore   60
The deed-mighty Scyldings,[4] did for the troopers
What best did avail them, and further moreover

---

[3] The rendering given in this translation represents the king as being
generous beyond the possibility of reproach; but some authorities construe
'him' (2996) as plu., and understand the passage to mean that no one
reproached the two brothers with having received more reward than they
were entitled to.

[4] The name 'Scyldingas' here (3006) has caused much discussion, and
given rise to several theories, the most important of which are as follows:
(1) After the downfall of Hrothgar's family, Beowulf was king of the Danes,
or Scyldings. (2) For 'Scyldingas' read 'Scylfingas'—that is, after killing
Eadgils, the Scylfing prince, Beowulf conquered his land, and held it in
subjection. (3) M. considers 3006 a thoughtless repetition of 2053.
(Cf. H.-So.)

It is time for us to pay the last marks of respect to our lord.
Hero-deeds 'complished. Now is haste most fitting,
That the lord of liegemen we look upon yonder,
And *that* one carry on journey to death-pyre   65
Who ring-presents gave us. Not aught of it all
Shall melt with the brave one—there's a mass of bright jewels,
Gold beyond measure, grewsomely purchased
And ending it all ornament-rings too
Bought with his life; these fire shall devour,   70
Flame shall cover, no earlman shall wear
A jewel-memento, nor beautiful virgin
Have on her neck rings to adorn her,
But wretched in spirit bereavèd of gold-gems
She shall oft with others be exiled and banished,   75
Since the leader of liegemen hath laughter forsaken,
Mirth and merriment. Hence many a war-spear
Cold from the morning shall be clutched in the fingers,
Heaved in the hand, no harp-music's sound shall
Waken the warriors, but the wan-coated raven   80
Fain over fey ones freely shall gabble,
Shall say to the eagle how he sped in the eating,
When, the wolf his companion, he plundered the slain.'
So the high-minded hero was rehearsing these stories
Loathsome to hear; he lied as to few of   85

The warriors go sadly to look at Beowulf's lifeless body.

Weirds and of words. All the war-troop arose then,
'Neath the Eagle's Cape sadly betook them,
Weeping and woful, the wonder to look at.
They saw on the sand then soulless a-lying,
His slaughter-bed holding, him who rings had given
          them   90
In days that were done; then the death-bringing moment
Was come to the good one, that the king very warlike,
Wielder of Weders, with wonder-death perished.
First they beheld there a creature more wondrous,

They also see the dragon.

The worm on the field, in front of them lying, 95
The foeman before them: the fire-spewing dragon,
Ghostly and grisly guest in his terrors,
Was scorched in the fire; as he lay there he measured
Fifty of feet; came forth in the night-time[5]
To rejoice in the air, thereafter departing 100
To visit his den; he in death was then fastened,
He would joy in no other earth-hollowed caverns.
There stood round about him beakers and vessels,
Dishes were lying and dear-valued weapons,
With iron-rust eaten, as in earth's mighty bosom 105
A thousand of winters there they had rested:

The hoard was under a magic spell.

That mighty bequest then with magic was guarded,
Gold of the ancients, that earlman not any
The ring-hall could touch, save Ruling-God only,
Sooth-king of Vict'ries gave whom He wished to 110

God alone could give access to it.

[6] (He is earth-folk's protector) to open the treasure,
E'en to such among mortals as seemed to Him proper.

[5] B. takes 'nihtes' and 'hwílum' (3045) as separate adverbial cases, and
renders: *Joy in the air had he of yore by night, etc.* He thinks that the idea
of vanished time ought to be expressed.

[6] The parenthesis is by some emended so as to read: (1) (*He* (i.e. *God*) *is
the hope of men*); (2) (*he is the hope of heroes*). Gr.'s reading has no parenthesis,
but says: . . . *could touch, unless God himself, true king of victories, gave to
whom he would to open the treasure, the secret place of enchanters, etc.* The
last is rejected on many grounds.

XLII.

Wiglaf's Sad Story—The Hoard Carried off

Then 'twas seen that the journey prospered him
    little
Who wrongly within had the ornaments hidden[1]
Down 'neath the wall. The warden erst slaughtered
Some few of the folk-troop: the feud then thereafter
Was hotly avengèd. 'Tis a wonder where,[2]   5
When the strength-famous trooper has attained to the end of
Life-days allotted, then no longer the man may
Remain with his kinsmen where mead-cups are flowing.
So to Beowulf happened when the ward of the barrow,

---

[1] For 'gehýdde,' B. suggests 'gehýðde': the passage would stand as above except the change of 'hidden' (v. 2) to 'plundered.' The reference, however, would be to the thief, not to the dragon.

[2] The passage 'Wundur . . . búan' (3063–3066), M. took to be a question asking whether it was strange that a man should die when his appointed time had come.—B. sees a corruption, and makes emendations introducing the idea that a brave man should not die from sickness or from old age, but should find death in the performance of some deed of daring.—S. sees an indirect question introduced by 'hwár' and dependent upon 'wundur': *A secret is it when the hero is to die, etc.*—Why may the two clauses not be parallel, and the whole passage an Old English cry of '*How wonderful is death!*'?—S.'s is the best yet offered, if 'wundor' means 'mystery.'

Assaults, he sought for: himself had no knowledge   10
How his leaving this life was likely to happen.
So to doomsday, famous folk-leaders down did
Call it with curses—who 'complished it there—
That that man should be ever of ill-deeds convicted,
Confined in foul-places, fastened in hell-bonds,   15
Punished with plagues, who this place should e'er ravage.[3]
He cared not for gold: rather the Wielder's
Favor preferred he first to get sight of.[4]

> Wiglaf addresses his comrades.

Wiglaf discoursed then, Wihstan his son:
'Oft many an earlman on one man's account must   20
Sorrow endure, as to us it hath happened.
The liegelord belovèd we could little prevail on,
Kingdom's keeper, counsel to follow,
Not to go to the guardian of the gold-hoard, but let him
Lie where he long was, live in his dwelling   25
Till the end of the world. Met we a destiny
Hard to endure: the hoard has been looked at,
Been gained very grimly; too grievous the fate that[5]
The prince of the people pricked to come thither.
I was therein and all of it looked at,   30
The building's equipments, since access was given me,
Not kindly at all entrance permitted

> He tells them of Beowulf's last moments.

Within under earth-wall. Hastily seized I
And held in my hands a huge-weighing burden
Of hoard-treasures costly, hither out bare them   35
To my liegelord belovèd: life was yet in him,

---

[3] For 'strude' in H.-So., S. suggests 'stride.' This would require 'ravage' (v. 16) to be changed to 'tread.'

[4] 'He cared . . . sight of' (17, 18), S. emends so as to read as follows: *He (Beowulf) had not before seen the favor of the avaricious possessor.*

[5] B. renders: *That which drew the king thither* (i.e. *the treasure*) *was granted us, but in such a way that it overcomes us.*

And consciousness also; the old one discoursed then
Much and mournfully, commanded to greet you,

> Beowulf's dying request.

Bade that remembering the deeds of your friend-lord
Ye build on the fire-hill of corpses a lofty   40
Burial-barrow, broad and far-famous,
As 'mid world-dwelling warriors he was widely most honored
While he reveled in riches. Let us rouse us and hasten
Again to see and seek for the treasure,
The wonder 'neath wall. The way I will show you,   45
That close ye may look at ring-gems sufficient
And gold in abundance. Let the bier with promptness
Fully be fashioned, when forth we shall come,
And lift we our lord, then, where long he shall tarry,
Well-beloved warrior, 'neath the Wielder's protection.' 50

> Wiglaf charges them to build a funeral-pyre.

Then the son of Wihstan bade orders be given,
Mood-valiant man, to many of heroes,
Holders of homesteads, that they hither from far,
[6]Leaders of liegemen, should look for the good one
With wood for his pyre: 'The flame shall now swallow   55
(The wan fire shall wax[7]) the warriors' leader
Who the rain of the iron often abided,
When, sturdily hurled, the storm of the arrows
Leapt o'er linden-wall, the lance rendered service,
Furnished with feathers followed the arrow.'   60
Now the wise-mooded son of Wihstan did summon
The best of the braves from the band of the ruler

---

[6] 'Folc-ágende' (3114) B. takes as dat. sing. with 'gódum,' and refers it to
Beowulf; that is, *Should bring fire-wood to the place where the good folk-ruler
lay.*

[7] C. proposes to take 'weaxan' = L. 'vescor,' and translate *devour.* This gives
a parallel to 'fretan' above. The parenthesis would be discarded and the
passage read: *Now shall the fire consume, the wan-flame devour, the prince
of warriors,* etc.

He takes seven thanes, and enters the den.

Seven together; 'neath the enemy's roof he
Went with the seven; one of the heroes
Who fared at the front, a fire-blazing torch-light   65
Bare in his hand. No lot then decided
Who that hoard should havoc, when hero-earls saw it
Lying in the cavern uncared-for entirely,
Rusting to ruin: they rued then but little
That they hastily hence hauled out the treasure,   70

They push the dragon over the wall.

The dear-valued jewels; the dragon eke pushed they,
The worm o'er the wall, let the wave-currents take him,
The waters enwind the ward of the treasures.

The hoard is laid on a wain.

There wounden gold on a wain was uploaded,
A mass unmeasured, the men-leader off then,   75
The hero hoary, to Whale's-Ness was carried.

XLIII.

The Burning of Beowulf

Beowulf's pyre.

The folk of the Geatmen got him then ready
A pile on the earth strong for the burning,
Behung with helmets, hero-knights' targets,
And bright-shining burnies, as he begged they should have
    them;
Then wailing war-heroes their world-famous chieftain,   5
Their liegelord beloved, laid in the middle.

The funeral-flame.

Soldiers began then to make on the barrow
The largest of dead-fires: dark o'er the vapor
The smoke-cloud ascended, the sad-roaring fire,
Mingled with weeping (the wind-roar subsided)   10
Till the building of bone it had broken to pieces,
Hot in the heart. Heavy in spirit
They mood-sad lamented the men-leader's ruin;
And mournful measures the much-grieving widow
* * * * * * *   15
* * * * * * *
* * * * * * *
* * * * * * *

* * * * * * *
* * * * * * *   20

> The Weders carry out their lord's last request.

The men of the Weders made accordingly
A hill on the height, high and extensive,
Of sea-going sailors to be seen from a distance,
And the brave one's beacon built where the fire was,
In ten-days' space, with a wall surrounded it,   25
As wisest of world-folk could most worthily plan it.
They placed in the barrow rings and jewels,

> Rings and gems are laid in the barrow.

All such ornaments as erst in the treasure
War-mooded men had won in possession:
The earnings of earlmen to earth they entrusted,   30
The gold to the dust, where yet it remaineth
As useless to mortals as in foregoing eras.
'Round the dead-mound rode then the doughty-in-battle,
Bairns of all twelve of the chiefs of the people,

> They mourn for their lord, and sing his praises.

More would they mourn, lament for their ruler,   35
Speak in measure, mention him with pleasure,
Weighed his worth, and his warlike achievements
Mightily commended, as 'tis meet one praise his
Liegelord in words and love him in spirit,
When forth from his body he fares to destruction.   40
So lamented mourning the men of the Geats,
Fond-loving vassals, the fall of their lord,

> An ideal king.

Said he was kindest of kings under heaven,
Gentlest of men, most winning of manner,
Friendliest to folk-troops and fondest of honor.   45

CLASSIC LITERATURE: WORDS AND PHRASES
adapted from the Collins English Dictionary

Accoucheur NOUN a male midwife or doctor ❑ *I think my sister must have had some general idea that I was a young offender whom an Accoucheur Policemen had taken up (on my birthday) and delivered over to her* (*Great Expectations* by Charles Dickens)

addled ADJ confused and unable to think properly ❑ *But she counted and counted till she got that addled* (*The Adventures of Huckleberry Finn* by Mark Twain)

admiration NOUN amazement or wonder ❑ *lifting up his hands and eyes by way of admiration* (*Gulliver's Travels* by Jonathan Swift)

afeard ADJ afeard means afraid ❑ *shake it–and don't be afeard* (*The Adventures of Huckleberry Finn* by Mark Twain)

affected VERB affected means followed ❑ *Hadst thou affected sweet divinity* (*Doctor Faustus 5.2* by Christopher Marlowe)

aground ADV when a boat runs aground, it touches the ground in a shallow part of the water and gets stuck ❑ *what kep' you?–boat get aground?* (*The Adventures of Huckleberry Finn* by Mark Twain)

ague NOUN a fever in which the patient has alternate hot and cold shivering fits ❑ *his exposure to the wet and cold had brought on fever and ague* (*Oliver Twist* by Charles Dickens)

alchemy ADJ false or worthless ❑ *all wealth alchemy* (*The Sun Rising* by John Donne)

all alike PHRASE the same all the time ❑ *Love, all alike* (*The Sun Rising* by John Donne)

alow and aloft PHRASE alow means in the lower part or bottom, and aloft means on the top, so alow and aloft means on the top and in the bottom or throughout ❑ *Someone's turned the chest out alow and aloft* (*Treasure Island* by Robert Louis Stevenson)

ambuscade NOUN ambuscade is not a proper word. Tom means an ambush, which is when a group of people attack their enemies, after hiding and waiting for them ❑ *and so we would lie in ambuscade, as he called it* (*The Adventures of Huckleberry Finn* by Mark Twain)

amiable ADJ likeable or pleasant ❑ *Such amiable qualities must speak for themselves* (*Pride and Prejudice* by Jane Austen)

amulet NOUN an amulet is a charm thought to drive away evil spirits. ❑ *uttered phrases at once occult and familiar, like the amulet worn on the heart* (*Silas Marner* by George Eliot)

amusement NOUN here amusement means a strange and disturbing puzzle ❑ *this was an amusement the other way* (*Robinson Crusoe* by Daniel Defoe)

ancient NOUN an ancient was the flag displayed on a ship to show which country it belongs to. It is also called the ensign ❑ *her ancient and pendants out* (*Robinson Crusoe* by Daniel Defoe)

antic ADJ here antic means horrible or grotesque ❑ *armed and dressed after a very antic manner* (*Gulliver's Travels* by Jonathan Swift)

antics NOUN antics is an old word meaning clowns, or people who do silly things to make other people laugh ❑ *And point like antics at his triple crown* (*Doctor Faustus 3.2* by Christopher Marlowe)

appanage NOUN an appanage is a living

allowance ❑ *As if loveliness were not the special prerogative of woman–her legitimate appanage and heritage!* (*Jane Eyre* by Charlotte Brontë)

appended VERB appended means attached or added to ❑ *and these words appended* (*Treasure Island* by Robert Louis Stevenson)

approver NOUN an approver is someone who gives evidence against someone he used to work with ❑ *Mr. Noah Claypole: receiving a free pardon from the Crown in consequence of being admitted approver against Fagin* (*Oliver Twist* by Charles Dickens)

areas NOUN the areas is the space, below street level, in front of the basement of a house ❑ *The Dodger had a vicious propensity, too, of pulling the caps from the heads of small boys and tossing them down areas* (*Oliver Twist* by Charles Dickens)

argument NOUN theme or important idea or subject which runs through a piece of writing ❑ *Thrice needful to the argument which now* (*The Prelude* by William Wordsworth)

artificially ADV artfully or cleverly ❑ *and he with a sharp flint sharpened very artificially* (*Gulliver's Travels* by Jonathan Swift)

artist NOUN here artist means a skilled workman ❑ *This man was a most ingenious artist* (*Gulliver's Travels* by Jonathan Swift)

assizes NOUN assizes were regular court sessions which a visiting judge was in charge of ❑ *you shall hang at the next assizes* (*Treasure Island* by Robert Louis Stevenson)

attraction NOUN gravitation, or Newton's theory of gravitation ❑ *he predicted the same fate to attraction* (*Gulliver's Travels* by Jonathan Swift)

aver VERB to aver is to claim something strongly ❑ *for Jem Rodney, the mole catcher, averred that one evening as he was returning homeward* (*Silas Marner* by George Eliot)

baby NOUN here baby means doll, which is a child's toy that looks like a small person ❑ *and skilful dressing her baby* (*Gulliver's Travels* by Jonathan Swift)

bagatelle NOUN bagatelle is a game rather like billiards and pool ❑ *Breakfast had been ordered at a pleasant little tavern, a mile or so away upon the rising ground beyond the green; and there was a bagatelle board in the room, in case we should desire to unbend our minds after the solemnity.* (*Great Expectations* by Charles Dickens)

bah EXCLAM Bah is an exclamation of frustration or anger ❑ *"Bah," said Scrooge.* (*A Christmas Carol* by Charles Dickens)

bairn NOUN a northern word for child ❑ *Who has taught you those fine words, my bairn?* (*Wuthering Heights* by Emily Brontë)

bait VERB to bait means to stop on a journey to take refreshment ❑ *So, when they stopped to bait the horse, and ate and drank and enjoyed themselves, I could touch nothing that they touched, but kept my fast unbroken.* (*David Copperfield* by Charles Dickens)

balustrade NOUN a balustrade is a row of vertical columns that form railings ❑ *but I mean to say you might have got a hearse up that staircase, and taken it broadwise, with the splinter-bar towards the wall, and the door towards the balustrades: and done it easy* (*A Christmas Carol* by Charles Dickens)

bandbox NOUN a large lightweight box for carrying bonnets or hats ❑ *I am glad I bought my bonnet, if it is only for the fun of having another bandbox* (*Pride and Prejudice* by Jane Austen)

barren NOUN a barren here is a stretch or expanse of barren land ❑ *a line of upright stones, continued the* *length of the barren* (*Wuthering Heights* by Emily Brontë)

basin NOUN a basin was a cup without a handle ❑ *who is drinking his tea out of a basin* (*Wuthering Heights* by Emily Brontë)

battalia NOUN the order of battle ❑ *till I saw part of his army in battalia* (*Gulliver's Travels* by Jonathan Swift)

battery NOUN a Battery is a fort or a place where guns are positioned ❑ *You bring the lot to me, at that old Battery over yonder* (*Great Expectations* by Charles Dickens)

battledore and shuttlecock NOUN The game battledore and shuttlecock was an early version of the game now known as badminton. The aim of the early game was simply to keep the shuttlecock from hitting the ground. ❑ *Battledore and shuttlecock's a wery good game vhen you an't the shuttlecock and two lawyers the battledores, in which case it gets too excitin' to be pleasant* (*Pickwick Papers* by Charles Dickens)

beadle NOUN a beadle was a local official who had power over the poor ❑ *But these impertinences were speedily checked by the evidence of the surgeon, and the testimony of the beadle* (*Oliver Twist* by Charles Dickens)

bearings NOUN the bearings of a place are the measurements or directions that are used to find or locate it ❑ *the bearings of the island* (*Treasure Island* by Robert Louis Stevenson)

beaufet NOUN a beaufet was a sideboard ❑ *and sweet-cake from the beaufet* (*Emma* by Jane Austen)

beck NOUN a beck is a small stream ❑ *a beck which follows the bend of the glen* (*Wuthering Heights* by Emily Brontë)

bedight VERB decorated ❑ *and bedight with Christmas holly stuck into the top.* (*A Christmas Carol* by Charles Dickens)

Bedlam NOUN Bedlam was a lunatic asylum in London which had statues carved by Caius Gabriel Cibber at its entrance ❑ *Bedlam, and those carved maniacs at the gates* (*The Prelude* by William Wordsworth)

beeves NOUN oxen or castrated bulls which are animals used for pulling vehicles or carrying things ❑ *to deliver in every morning six beeves* (*Gulliver's Travels* by Jonathan Swift)

begot VERB created or caused ❑ *Begot in thee* (*On His Mistress* by John Donne)

behoof NOUN behoof means benefit ❑ *"Yes, young man," said he, releasing the handle of the article in question, retiring a step or two from my table, and speaking for the behoof of the landlord and waiter at the door* (*Great Expectations* by Charles Dickens)

berth NOUN a berth is a bed on a boat ❑ *this is the berth for me* (*Treasure Island* by Robert Louis Stevenson)

bevers NOUN a bever was a snack, or small portion of food, eaten between main meals ❑ *that buys me thirty meals a day and ten bevers* (*Doctor Faustus 2.1* by Christopher Marlowe)

bilge water NOUN the bilge is the widest part of a ship's bottom, and the bilge water is the dirty water that collects there ❑ *no gush of bilge-water had turned it to fetid puddle* (*Jane Eyre* by Charlotte Brontë)

bills NOUN bills is an old term meaning prescription. A prescription is the piece of paper on which your doctor writes an order for medicine and which you give to a chemist to get the medicine ❑ *Are not thy bills hung up as monuments* (*Doctor Faustus 1.1* by Christopher Marlowe)

black cap NOUN a judge wore a black cap when he was about to sentence a prisoner to death ❑ *The judge assumed the black cap, and the* *prisoner still stood with the same air and gesture.* (*Oliver Twist* by Charles Dickens)

black gentleman NOUN this was another word for the devil ❑ *for she is as impatient as the black gentleman* (*Emma* by Jane Austen)

boot-jack NOUN a wooden device to help take boots off ❑ *The speaker appeared to throw a boot-jack, or some such article, at the person he addressed* (*Oliver Twist* by Charles Dickens)

booty NOUN booty means treasure or prizes ❑ *would be inclined to give up their booty in payment of the dead man's debts* (*Treasure Island* by Robert Louis Stevenson)

Bow Street runner PHRASE Bow Street runners were the first British police force, set up by the author Henry Fielding in the eighteenth century ❑ *as would have convinced a judge or a Bow Street runner* (*Treasure Island* by Robert Louis Stevenson)

brawn NOUN brawn is a dish of meat which is set in jelly ❑ *Heaped up upon the floor, to form a kind of throne, were turkeys, geese, game, poultry, brawn, great joints of meat, sucking-pigs* (*A Christmas Carol* by Charles Dickens)

bray VERB when a donkey brays, it makes a loud, harsh sound ❑ *and she doesn't bray like a jackass* (*The Adventures of Huckleberry Finn* by Mark Twain)

break VERB in order to train a horse you first have to break it ❑ *"If a high-mettled creature like this," said he, "can't be broken by fair means, she will never be good for anything"* (*Black Beauty* by Anna Sewell)

bullyragging VERB bullyragging is an old word which means bullying. To bullyrag someone is to threaten or force someone to do something they don't want to do ❑ *and a lot of loafers bullyragging him for sport* (*The Adventures of Huckleberry Finn* by Mark Twain)

but PREP except for (this) ❑ *but this, all pleasures fancies be* (*The Good-Morrow* by John Donne)

by hand PHRASE by hand was a common expression of the time meaning that baby had been fed either using a spoon or a bottle rather than by breast-feeding ❑ *My sister, Mrs. Joe Gargery, was more than twenty years older than I, and had established a great reputation with herself . . . because she had bought me up 'by hand'* (*Great Expectations* by Charles Dickens)

bye-spots NOUN bye-spots are lonely places ❑ *and bye-spots of tales rich with indigenous produce* (*The Prelude* by William Wordsworth)

calico NOUN calico is plain white fabric made from cotton ❑ *There was two old dirty calico dresses* (*The Adventures of Huckleberry Finn* by Mark Twain)

camp-fever NOUN camp-fever was another word for the disease typhus ❑ *during a severe camp-fever* (*Emma* by Jane Austen)

cant NOUN cant is insincere or empty talk ❑ *"Man," said the Ghost, "if man you be in heart, not adamant, forbear that wicked cant until you have discovered What the surplus is, and Where it is."* (*A Christmas Carol* by Charles Dickens)

canty ADJ canty means lively, full of life ❑ *My mother lived til eighty, a canty dame to the last* (*Wuthering Heights* by Emily Brontë)

canvas VERB to canvas is to discuss ❑ *We think so very differently on this point Mr Knightley, that there can be no use in canvassing it* (*Emma* by Jane Austen)

capital ADJ capital means excellent or extremely good ❑ *for it's capital, so shady, light, and big* (*Little Women* by Louisa May Alcott)

capstan NOUN a capstan is a device used on a ship to lift sails and anchors ❑ *capstans going, ships going out to sea, and unintelligible* *sea creatures roaring curses over the bulwarks at respondent lightermen* (*Great Expectations* by Charles Dickens)

case-bottle NOUN a square bottle designed to fit with others into a case ❑ *The spirit being set before him in a huge case-bottle, which had originally come out of some ship's locker* (*The Old Curiosity Shop* by Charles Dickens)

casement NOUN casement is a word meaning window. The teacher in *Nicholas Nickleby* misspells window showing what a bad teacher he is ❑ *W-i-n, win, d-e-r, der, winder, a casement.* (*Nicholas Nickleby* by Charles Dickens)

cataleptic ADJ a cataleptic fit is one in which the victim goes into a trance-like state and remains still for a long time ❑ *It was at this point in their history that Silas's cataleptic fit occurred during the prayer-meeting* (*Silas Marner* by George Eliot)

cauldron NOUN a cauldron is a large cooking pot made of metal ❑ *stirring a large cauldron which seemed to be full of soup* (*Alice's Adventures in Wonderland* by Lewis Carroll)

cephalic ADJ cephalic means to do with the head ❑ *with ink composed of a cephalic tincture* (*Gulliver's Travels* by Jonathan Swift)

chaise and four NOUN a closed four-wheel carriage pulled by four horses ❑ *he came down on Monday in a chaise and four to see the place* (*Pride and Prejudice* by Jane Austen)

chamberlain NOUN the main servant in a household ❑ *In those times a bed was always to be got there at any hour of the night, and the chamberlain, letting me in at his ready wicket, lighted the candle next in order on his shelf* (*Great Expectations* by Charles Dickens)

characters NOUN distinguishing marks ❑ *Impressed upon all forms the characters* (*The Prelude* by William Wordsworth)

chary ADJ cautious ❑ *I should have been chary of discussing my guardian too freely even with her* (*Great Expectations* by Charles Dickens)

cherishes VERB here cherishes means cheers or brightens ❑ *some philosophic song of Truth that cherishes our daily life* (*The Prelude* by William Wordsworth)

chickens' meat PHRASE chickens' meat is an old term which means chickens' feed or food ❑ *I had shook a bag of chickens' meat out in that place* (*Robinson Crusoe* by Daniel Defoe)

chimeras NOUN a chimera is an unrealistic idea or a wish which is unlikely to be fulfilled ❑ *with many other wild impossible chimeras* (*Gulliver's Travels* by Jonathan Swift)

chines NOUN chine is a cut of meat that includes part or all of the backbone of the animal ❑ *and they found hams and chines uncut* (*Silas Marner* by George Eliot)

chits NOUN chits is a slang word which means girls ❑ *I hate affected, niminy-piminy chits!* (*Little Women* by Louisa May Alcott)

chopped VERB chopped means come suddenly or accidentally ❑ *if I had chopped upon them* (*Robinson Crusoe* by Daniel Defoe)

chute NOUN a narrow channel ❑ *One morning about day-break, I found a canoe and crossed over a chute to the main shore* (*The Adventures of Huckleberry Finn* by Mark Twain)

circumspection NOUN careful observation of events and circumstances; caution ❑ *I honour your circumspection* (*Pride and Prejudice* by Jane Austen)

clambered VERB clambered means to climb somewhere with difficulty, usually using your hands and your feet ❑ *he clambered up and down stairs* (*Treasure Island* by Robert Louis Stevenson)

clime NOUN climate ❏ *no season knows nor clime* (*The Sun Rising* by John Donne)

clinched VERB clenched ❏ *the tops whereof I could but just reach with my fist clinched* (*Gulliver's Travels* by Jonathan Swift)

close chair NOUN a close chair is a sedan chair, which is an covered chair which has room for one person. The sedan chair is carried on two poles by two men, one in front and one behind ❏ *persuaded even the Empress herself to let me hold her in her close chair* (*Gulliver's Travels* by Jonathan Swift)

clown NOUN clown here means peasant or person who lives off the land ❏ *In ancient days by emperor and clown* (*Ode on a Nightingale* by John Keats)

coalheaver NOUN a coalheaver loaded coal onto ships using a spade ❏ *Good, strong, wholesome medicine, as was given with great success to two Irish labourers and a coalheaver* (*Oliver Twist* by Charles Dickens)

coal-whippers NOUN men who worked at docks using machines to load coal onto ships ❏ *here, were colliers by the score and score, with the coal-whippers plunging off stages on deck* (*Great Expectations* by Charles Dickens)

cobweb NOUN a cobweb is the net which a spider makes for catching insects ❏ *the walls and ceilings were all hung round with cobwebs* (*Gulliver's Travels* by Jonathan Swift)

coddling VERB coddling means to treat someone too kindly or protect them too much ❏ *and I've been coddling the fellow as if I'd been his grand-mother* (*Little Women* by Louisa May Alcott)

coil NOUN coil means noise or fuss or disturbance ❏ *What a coil is there?* (*Doctor Faustus 4.7* by Christopher Marlowe)

collared VERB to collar something is a slang term which means to capture. In this sentence, it means he stole it [the money] ❏ *he collared it* (*The Adventures of Huckleberry Finn* by Mark Twain)

colling VERB colling is an old word which means to embrace and kiss ❏ *and no clasping and colling at all* (*Tess of the D'Urbervilles* by Thomas Hardy)

colloquies NOUN colloquy is a formal conversation or dialogue ❏ *Such colloquies have occupied many a pair of pale-faced weavers* (*Silas Marner* by George Eliot)

comfit NOUN sugar-covered pieces of fruit or nut eaten as sweets ❏ *and pulled out a box of comfits* (*Alice's Adventures in Wonderland* by Lewis Carroll)

coming out VERB when a girl came out in society it meant she was of marriageable age. In order to 'come out' girls were expecting to attend balls and other parties during a season ❏ *The younger girls formed hopes of coming out a year or two sooner than they might otherwise have done* (*Pride and Prejudice* by Jane Austen)

commit VERB commit means arrest or stop ❏ *Commit the rascals* (*Doctor Faustus 4.7* by Christopher Marlowe)

commodious ADJ commodious means convenient ❏ *the most commodious and effectual ways* (*Gulliver's Travels* by Jonathan Swift)

commons NOUN commons is an old term meaning food shared with others ❏ *his pauper assistants ranged them-selves behind him; the gruel was served out; and a long grace was said over the short commons.* (*Oliver Twist* by Charles Dickens)

complacency NOUN here complacency means a desire to please others. To-day complacency means feeling pleased with oneself without good reason. ❏ *Twas thy power that raised the first complacency in me* (*The Prelude* by William Wordsworth)

complaisance NOUN complaisance was eagerness to please ❑ *we cannot wonder at his complaisance* (*Pride and Prejudice* by Jane Austen)

complaisant ADJ complaisant means polite ❑ *extremely cheerful and complaisant to their guest* (*Gulliver's Travels* by Jonathan Swift)

conning VERB conning means learning by heart ❑ *Or conning more* (*The Prelude* by William Wordsworth)

consequent NOUN consequence ❑ *as avarice is the necessary consequent of old age* (*Gulliver's Travels* by Jonathan Swift)

consorts NOUN concerts ❑ *The King, who delighted in music, had frequent consorts at Court* (*Gulliver's Travels* by Jonathan Swift)

conversible ADJ conversible meant easy to talk to, companionable ❑ *He can be a conversible companion* (*Pride and Prejudice* by Jane Austen)

copper NOUN a copper is a large pot that can be heated directly over a fire ❑ *He gazed in stupefied astonishment on the small rebel for some seconds, and then clung for support to the copper* (*Oliver Twist* by Charles Dickens)

copper-stick NOUN a copper-stick is the long piece of wood used to stir washing in the copper (or boiler) which was usually the biggest cooking pot in the house ❑ *It was Christmas Eve, and I had to stir the pudding for next day, with a copper-stick, from seven to eight by the Dutch clock* (*Great Expectations* by Charles Dickens)

counting-house NOUN a counting-house is a place where accountants work ❑ *Once upon a time–of all the good days in the year, on Christmas Eve–old Scrooge sat busy in his counting-house* (*A Christmas Carol* by Charles Dickens)

courtier NOUN a courtier is someone who attends the king or queen–a member of the court ❑ *next the ten courtiers;* (*Alice's Adventures in Wonderland* by Lewis Carroll)

covies NOUN covies were flocks of partridges ❑ *and will save all of the best covies for you* (*Pride and Prejudice* by Jane Austen)

cowed VERB cowed means frightened or intimidated ❑ *it cowed me more than the pain* (*Treasure Island* by Robert Louis Stevenson)

cozened VERB cozened means tricked or deceived ❑ *Do you remember, sir, how you cozened me* (*Doctor Faustus 4.7* by Christopher Marlowe)

cravats NOUN a cravat is a folded cloth that a man wears wrapped around his neck as a decorative item of clothing ❑ *we'd 'a' slept in our cravats to-night* (*The Adventures of Huckleberry Finn* by Mark Twain)

crock and dirt PHRASE crock and dirt is an old expression meaning soot and dirt ❑ *and the mare catching cold at the door, and the boy grimed with crock and dirt* (*Great Expectations* by Charles Dickens)

crockery NOUN here crockery means pottery ❑ *By one of the parrots was a cat made of crockery* (*The Adventures of Huckleberry Finn* by Mark Twain)

crooked sixpence PHRASE it was considered unlucky to have a bent sixpence ❑ *You've got the beauty, you see, and I've got the luck, so you must keep me by you for your crooked sixpence* (*Silas Marner* by George Eliot)

croquet NOUN croquet is a traditional English summer game in which players try to hit wooden balls through hoops ❑ *and once she remembered trying to box her own ears for having cheated herself in a game of croquet* (*Alice's Adventures in Wonderland* by Lewis Carroll)

cross PREP across ❑ *The two great streets, which run cross and divide it into four quarters* (*Gulliver's Travels* by Jonathan Swift)

culpable ADJ if you are culpable for something it means you are to blame ❏ *deep are the sorrows that spring from false ideas for which no man is culpable.* (*Silas Marner* by George Eliot)

cultured ADJ cultivated ❏ *Nor less when spring had warmed the cultured Vale* (*The Prelude* by William Wordsworth)

cupidity NOUN cupidity is greed ❏ *These people hated me with the hatred of cupidity and disappointment.* (*Great Expectations* by Charles Dickens)

curricle NOUN an open two-wheeled carriage with one seat for the driver and space for a single passenger ❏ *and they saw a lady and a gentleman in a curricle* (*Pride and Prejudice* by Jane Austen)

cynosure NOUN a cynosure is something that strongly attracts attention or admiration ❏ *Then I thought of Eliza and Georgiana; I beheld one the cynosure of a ballroom, the other the inmate of a convent cell* (*Jane Eyre* by Charlotte Brontë)

dalliance NOUN someone's dalliance with something is a brief involvement with it ❏ *nor sporting in the dalliance of love* (*Doctor Faustus Chorus* by Christopher Marlowe)

darkling ADV darkling is an archaic way of saying in the dark ❏ *Darkling I listen* (*Ode on a Nightingale* by John Keats)

delf-case NOUN a sideboard for holding dishes and crockery ❏ *at the pewter dishes and delf-case* (*Wuthering Heights* by Emily Brontë)

determined ■ VERB here determined means ended ❏ *and be out of vogue when that was determined* (*Gulliver's Travels* by Jonathan Swift) ■ VERB determined can mean to have been learned or found especially by investigation or experience ❏ *All the sensitive feelings it wounded so cruelly, all the shame and misery it kept alive within my breast, became more poignant as I*

thought of this; and I determined that the life was unendurable (*David Copperfield* by Charles Dickens)

Deuce NOUN a slang term for the Devil ❏ *Ah, I dare say I did. Deuce take me, he added suddenly, I know I did. I find I am not quite unscrewed yet.* (*Great Expectations* by Charles Dickens)

diabolical ADJ diabolical means devilish or evil ❏ *and with a thousand diabolical expressions* (*Treasure Island* by Robert Louis Stevenson)

direction NOUN here direction means address ❏ *Elizabeth was not surprised at it, as Jane had written the direction remarkably ill* (*Pride and Prejudice* by Jane Austen)

discover VERB to make known or announce ❏ *the Emperor would discover the secret while I was out of his power* (*Gulliver's Travels* by Jonathan Swift)

dissemble VERB hide or conceal ❏ *Dissemble nothing* (*On His Mistress* by John Donne)

dissolve VERB dissolve here means to release from life, to die ❏ *Fade far away, dissolve, and quite forget* (*Ode on a Nightingale* by John Keats)

distrain VERB to distrain is to seize the property of someone who is in debt in compensation for the money owed ❏ *for he's threatening to distrain for it* (*Silas Marner* by George Eliot)

Divan NOUN a Divan was originally a Turkish council of state–the name was transferred to the couches they sat on and is used to mean this in English ❏ *Mr Brass applauded this picture very much, and the bed being soft and comfortable, Mr Quilp determined to use it, both as a sleeping place by night and as a kind of Divan by day.* (*The Old Curiosity Shop* by Charles Dickens)

divorcement NOUN separation ❏ *By all pains which want and divorcement* *hath* (*On His Mistress* by John Donne)

dog in the manger, PHRASE this phrase describes someone who prevents you from enjoying something that they themselves have no need for ❑ *You are a dog in the manger, Cathy, and desire no one to be loved but yourself* (*Wuthering Heights* by Emily Brontë)

dolorifuge NOUN dolorifuge is a word which Thomas Hardy invented. It means pain-killer or comfort ❑ *as a species of dolorifuge* (*Tess of the D'Urbervilles* by Thomas Hardy)

dome NOUN building ❑ *that river and that mouldering dome* (*The Prelude* by William Wordsworth)

domestic NOUN here domestic means a person's management of the house ❑ *to give some account of my domestic* (*Gulliver's Travels* by Jonathan Swift)

dunce NOUN a dunce is another word for idiot ❑ *Do you take me for a dunce? Go on?* (*Alice's Adventures in Wonderland* by Lewis Carroll)

Ecod EXCLAM a slang exclamation meaning 'oh God!' ❑ *"Ecod," replied Wemmick, shaking his head, "that's not my trade."* (*Great Expectations* by Charles Dickens)

egg-hot NOUN an egg-hot (see also 'flip' and 'negus') was a hot drink made from beer and eggs, sweetened with nutmeg ❑ *She fainted when she saw me return, and made a little jug of egg-hot afterwards to console us while we talked it over.* (*David Copperfield* by Charles Dickens)

encores NOUN an encore is a short extra performance at the end of a longer one, which the entertainer gives because the audience has enthusiastically asked for it ❑ *we want a little something to answer encores with, anyway* (*The Adventures of Huckleberry Finn* by Mark Twain)

equipage NOUN an elegant and impressive carriage ❑ *and besides, the equipage did not answer to any of*

their neighbours (*Pride and Prejudice* by Jane Austen)

exordium NOUN an exordium is the opening part of a speech ❑ *"Now, Handel," as if it were the grave beginning of a portentous business exordium, he had suddenly given up that tone* (*Great Expectations* by Charles Dickens)

expect VERB here expect means to wait for ❑ *to expect his farther commands* (*Gulliver's Travels* by Jonathan Swift)

familiars NOUN familiars means spirits or devils who come to someone when they are called ❑ *I'll turn all the lice about thee into familiars* (*Doctor Faustus 1.4* by Christopher Marlowe)

fantods NOUN a fantod is a person who fidgets or can't stop moving nervously ❑ *It most give me the fantods* (*The Adventures of Huckleberry Finn* by Mark Twain)

farthing NOUN a farthing is an old unit of British currency which was worth a quarter of a penny ❑ *Not a farthing less. A great many back-payments are included in it, I assure you.* (*A Christmas Carol* by Charles Dickens)

farthingale NOUN a hoop worn under a skirt to extend it ❑ *A bell with an old voice–which I dare say in its time had often said to the house, Here is the green farthingale* (*Great Expectations* by Charles Dickens)

favours NOUN here favours is an old word which means ribbons ❑ *A group of humble mourners entered the gate: wearing white favours* (*Oliver Twist* by Charles Dickens)

feigned VERB pretend or pretending ❑ *not my feigned page* (*On His Mistress* by John Donne)

fence ■ NOUN a fence is someone who receives and sells stolen goods ❑ *What are you up to? Ill-treating the boys, you covetous, avaricious, in-sa-ti-a-ble old fence?* (*Oliver Twist* by

Charles Dickens) ■ NOUN defence or protection ❏ *but honesty hath no fence against superior cunning* (*Gulliver's Travels* by Jonathan Swift)

fess ADJ fess is an old word which means pleased or proud ❏ *You'll be fess enough, my poppet* (*Tess of the D'Urbervilles* by Thomas Hardy)

fettered ADJ fettered means bound in chains or chained ❏ *"You are fettered," said Scrooge, trembling. "Tell me why?"* (*A Christmas Carol* by Charles Dickens)

fidges VERB fidges means fidgets, which is to keep moving your hands slightly because you are nervous or excited ❏ *Look, Jim, how my fingers fidges* (*Treasure Island* by Robert Louis Stevenson)

finger-post NOUN a finger-post is a sign-post showing the direction to different places ❏ *"The gallows," continued Fagin, "the gallows, my dear, is an ugly finger-post, which points out a very short and sharp turning that has stopped many a bold fellow's career on the broad highway."* (*Oliver Twist* by Charles Dickens)

fire-irons NOUN fire-irons are tools kept by the side of the fire to either cook with or look after the fire ❏ *the fire-irons came first* (*Alice's Adventures in Wonderland* by Lewis Carroll)

fire-plug NOUN a fire-plug is another word for a fire hydrant ❏ *The pony looked with great attention into a fire-plug, which was near him, and appeared to be quite absorbed in contemplating it* (*The Old Curiosity Shop* by Charles Dickens)

flank NOUN flank is the side of an animal ❏ *And all her silken flanks with garlands dressed* (*Ode on a Grecian Urn* by John Keats)

flip NOUN a flip is a drink made from warmed ale, sugar, spice and beaten egg ❏ *The events of the day, in combination with the twins, if not with the flip, had made Mrs.*

Micawber hysterical, and she shed tears as she replied (*David Copperfield* by Charles Dickens)

flit VERB flit means to move quickly ❏ *and if he had meant to flit to Thrushcross Grange* (*Wuthering Heights* by Emily Brontë)

floorcloth NOUN a floorcloth was a hard-wearing piece of canvas used instead of carpet ❏ *This avenging phantom was ordered to be on duty at eight on Tuesday morning in the hall (it was two feet square, as charged for floorcloth)* (*Great Expectations* by Charles Dickens)

fly-driver NOUN a fly-driver is a carriage drawn by a single horse ❏ *The fly-drivers, among whom I inquired next, were equally jocose and equally disrespectful* (*David Copperfield* by Charles Dickens)

fob NOUN a small pocket in which a watch is kept ❏ *"Certain," replied the man, drawing a gold watch from his fob* (*Oliver Twist* by Charles Dickens)

folly NOUN folly means foolishness or stupidity ❏ *the folly of beginning a work* (*Robinson Crusoe* by Daniel Defoe)

fond ADJ fond means foolish ❏ *Fond worldling* (*Doctor Faustus 5.2* by Christopher Marlowe)

fondness NOUN silly or foolish affection ❏ *They have no fondness for their colts or foals* (*Gulliver's Travels* by Jonathan Swift)

for his fancy PHRASE for his fancy means for his liking or as he wanted ❏ *and as I did not obey quick enough for his fancy* (*Treasure Island* by Robert Louis Stevenson)

forlorn ADJ lost or very upset ❏ *you are from that day forlorn* (*Gulliver's Travels* by Jonathan Swift)

foster-sister NOUN a foster-sister was someone brought up by the same nurse or in the same household ❏ *I had been his foster-sister* (*Wuthering Heights* by Emily Brontë)

fox-fire NOUN fox-fire is a weak glow that is given off by decaying, rotten wood ❑ *what we must have was a lot of them rotten chunks that's called fox-fire* (*The Adventures of Huckleberry Finn* by Mark Twain)

frozen sea PHRASE the Arctic Ocean ❑ *into the frozen sea* (*Gulliver's Travels* by Jonathan Swift)

gainsay VERB to gainsay something is to say it isn't true or to deny it ❑ *"So she had," cried Scrooge. "You're right. I'll not gainsay it, Spirit. God forbid!"* (*A Christmas Carol* by Charles Dickens)

gaiters NOUN gaiters were leggings made of a cloth or piece of leather which covered the leg from the knee to the ankle ❑ *Mr Knightley was hard at work upon the lower buttons of his thick leather gaiters* (*Emma* by Jane Austen)

galluses NOUN galluses is an old spelling of gallows, and here means suspenders. Suspenders are straps worn over someone's shoulders and fastened to their trousers to prevent the trousers falling down ❑ *and home-knit galluses* (*The Adventures of Huckleberry Finn* by Mark Twain)

galoot NOUN a sailor but also a clumsy person ❑ *and maybe a galoot on it chopping* (*The Adventures of Huckleberry Finn* by Mark Twain)

gayest ADJ gayest means the most lively and bright or merry ❑ *Beth played her gayest march* (*Little Women* by Louisa May Alcott)

gem NOUN here gem means jewellery ❑ *the mountain shook off turf and flower, had only heath for raiment and crag for gem* (*Jane Eyre* by Charlotte Brontë)

giddy ADJ giddy means dizzy ❑ *and I wish you wouldn't keep appearing and vanishing so suddenly; you make one quite giddy.* (*Alice's Adventures in Wonderland* by Lewis Carroll)

gig NOUN a light two-wheeled carriage ❑ *when a gig drove up to the garden gate: out of which there jumped a fat gentleman* (*Oliver Twist* by Charles Dickens)

gladsome ADJ gladsome is an old word meaning glad or happy ❑ *Nobody ever stopped him in the street to say, with gladsome looks* (*A Christmas Carol* by Charles Dickens)

glen NOUN a glen is a small valley; the word is used commonly in Scotland ❑ *a beck which follows the bend of the glen* (*Wuthering Heights* by Emily Brontë)

gravelled VERB gravelled is an old term which means to baffle or defeat someone ❑ *Gravelled the pastors of the German Church* (*Doctor Faustus 1.1* by Christopher Marlowe)

grinder NOUN a grinder was a private tutor ❑ *but that when he had had the happiness of marrying Mrs Pocket very early in his life, he had impaired his prospects and taken up the calling of a Grinder* (*Great Expectations* by Charles Dickens)

gruel NOUN gruel is a thin, watery cornmeal or oatmeal soup ❑ *and the little saucepan of gruel (Scrooge had a cold in his head) upon the hob.* (*A Christmas Carol* by Charles Dickens)

guinea, half a NOUN half a guinea was ten shillings and sixpence ❑ *but lay out half a guinea at Ford's* (*Emma* by Jane Austen)

gull VERB gull is an old term which means to fool or deceive someone ❑ *Hush, I'll gull him supernaturally* (*Doctor Faustus 3.4* by Christopher Marlowe)

gunnel NOUN the gunnel, or gunwale, is the upper edge of a boat's side ❑ *But he put his foot on the gunnel and rocked her* (*The Adventures of Huckleberry Finn* by Mark Twain)

gunwale NOUN the side of a ship ❑ *He dipped his hand in the water over the boat's gunwale* (*Great Expectations* by Charles Dickens)

Gytrash NOUN a Gytrash is an omen of misfortune to the superstitious, usually taking the form of a hound ❏ *I remembered certain of Bessie's tales, wherein figured a North-of-England spirit, called a 'Gytrash'* (*Jane Eyre* by Charlotte Brontë)

hackney-cabriolet NOUN a two-wheeled carriage with four seats for hire and pulled by a horse ❏ *A hackney-cabriolet was in waiting; with the same vehemence which she had exhibited in addressing Oliver, the girl pulled him in with her, and drew the curtains close.* (*Oliver Twist* by Charles Dickens)

hackney-coach NOUN a four-wheeled horse-drawn vehicle for hire ❏ *The twilight was beginning to close in, when Mr. Brownlow alighted from a hackney-coach at his own door, and knocked softly.* (*Oliver Twist* by Charles Dickens)

haggler NOUN a haggler is someone who travels from place to place selling small goods and items ❏ *when I be plain Jack Durbeyfield, the haggler* (*Tess of the D'Urbervilles* by Thomas Hardy)

halter NOUN a halter is a rope or strap used to lead an animal or to tie it up ❏ *I had of course long been used to a halter and a headstall* (*Black Beauty* by Anna Sewell)

hamlet NOUN a hamlet is a small village or a group of houses in the countryside ❏ *down from the hamlet* (*Treasure Island* by Robert Louis Stevenson)

hand-barrow NOUN a hand-barrow is a device for carrying heavy objects. It is like a wheelbarrow except that it has handles, rather than wheels, for moving the barrow ❏ *his sea chest following behind him in a hand-barrow* (*Treasure Island* by Robert Louis Stevenson)

handspike NOUN a handspike was a stick which was used as a lever ❏ *a bit of stick like a handspike* (*Treasure Island* by Robert Louis Stevenson)

haply ADV haply means by chance or perhaps ❏ *And haply the Queen-Moon is on her throne* (*Ode on a Nightingale* by John Keats)

harem NOUN the harem was the part of the house where the women lived ❏ *mostly they hang round the harem* (*The Adventures of Huckleberry Finn* by Mark Twain)

hautboys NOUN hautboys are oboes ❏ *sausages and puddings resembling flutes and hautboys* (*Gulliver's Travels* by Jonathan Swift)

hawker NOUN a hawker is someone who sells goods to people as he travels rather than from a fixed place like a shop ❏ *to buy some stockings from a hawker* (*Treasure Island* by Robert Louis Stevenson)

hawser NOUN a hawser is a rope used to tie up or tow a ship or boat ❏ *Again among the tiers of shipping, in and out, avoiding rusty chain-cables, frayed hempen hawsers* (*Great Expectations* by Charles Dickens)

headstall NOUN the headstall is the part of the bridle or halter that goes around a horse's head ❏ *I had of course long been used to a halter and a headstall* (*Black Beauty* by Anna Sewell)

hearken VERB hearken means to listen ❏ *though we sometimes stopped to lay hold of each other and hearken* (*Treasure Island* by Robert Louis Stevenson)

heartless ADJ here heartless means without heart or dejected ❏ *I am not heartless* (*The Prelude* by William Wordsworth)

hebdomadal ADJ hebdomadal means weekly ❏ *It was the hebdomadal treat to which we all looked forward from Sabbath to Sabbath* (*Jane Eyre* by Charlotte Brontë)

highwaymen NOUN highwaymen were people who stopped travellers and robbed them ❏ *We are high-waymen* (*The Adventures of Huckleberry Finn* by Mark Twain)

hinds NOUN hinds means farm hands, or people who work on a farm ❑ *He called his hinds about him* (*Gulliver's Travels* by Jonathan Swift)

histrionic ADJ if you refer to someone's behaviour as histrionic, you are being critical of it because it is dramatic and exaggerated ❑ *But the histrionic muse is the darling* (*The Adventures of Huckleberry Finn* by Mark Twain)

hogs NOUN hogs is another word for pigs ❑ *Tom called the hogs 'ingots'* (*The Adventures of Huckleberry Finn* by Mark Twain)

horrors NOUN the horrors are a fit, called delirium tremens, which is caused by drinking too much alcohol ❑ *I'll have the horrors* (*Treasure Island* by Robert Louis Stevenson)

huffy ADJ huffy means to be obviously annoyed or offended about something ❑ *They will feel that more than angry speeches or huffy actions* (*Little Women* by Louisa May Alcott)

hulks NOUN hulks were prison-ships ❑ *The miserable companion of thieves and ruffians, the fallen outcast of low haunts, the associate of the scourings of the jails and hulks* (*Oliver Twist* by Charles Dickens)

humbug NOUN humbug means nonsense or rubbish ❑ *"Bah," said Scrooge. "Humbug!"* (*A Christmas Carol* by Charles Dickens)

humours NOUN it was believed that there were four fluids in the body called humours which decided the temperament of a person depending on how much of each fluid was present ❑ *other peccant humours* (*Gulliver's Travels* by Jonathan Swift)

husbandry NOUN husbandry is farming animals ❑ *bad husbandry were plentifully anointing their wheels* (*Silas Marner* by George Eliot)

huswife NOUN a huswife was a small sewing kit ❑ *but I had put my huswife on it* (*Emma* by Jane Austen)

ideal ADJ ideal in this context means imaginary ❑ *I discovered the yell was not ideal* (*Wuthering Heights* by Emily Brontë)

If our two PHRASE if both our ❑ *If our two loves be one* (*The Good-Morrow* by John Donne)

ignis-fatuus NOUN ignis-fatuus is the light given out by burning marsh gases, which lead careless travellers into danger ❑ *it is madness in all women to let a secret love kindle within them, which, if unreturned and unknown, must devour the life that feeds it; and, if discovered and responded to, must lead ignis-fatuus-like, into miry wilds whence there is no extrication.* (*Jane Eyre* by Charlotte Brontë)

imaginations NOUN here imaginations means schemes or plans ❑ *soon drove out those imaginations* (*Gulliver's Travels* by Jonathan Swift)

impressible ADJ impressible means open or impressionable ❑ *for Marner had one of those impressible, self-doubting natures* (*Silas Marner* by George Eliot)

in good intelligence PHRASE friendly with each other ❑ *that these two persons were in good intelligence with each other* (*Gulliver's Travels* by Jonathan Swift)

inanity NOUN inanity is silliness or dull stupidity ❑ *Do we not wile away moments of inanity* (*Silas Marner* by George Eliot)

incivility NOUN incivility means rudeness or impoliteness ❑ *if it's only for a piece of incivility like to-night's* (*Treasure Island* by Robert Louis Stevenson)

indigenae NOUN indigenae means natives or people from that area ❑ *an exotic that the surly indigenae will not recognise for kin* (*Wuthering Heights* by Emily Brontë)

indocible ADJ unteachable ❑ *so they were the most restive and indocible* (*Gulliver's Travels* by Jonathan Swift)

ingenuity NOUN inventiveness ❏ *entreated me to give him something as an encouragement to ingenuity* (*Gulliver's Travels* by Jonathan Swift)

ingots NOUN an ingot is a lump of a valuable metal like gold, usually shaped like a brick ❏ *Tom called the hogs 'ingots'* (*The Adventures of Huckleberry Finn* by Mark Twain)

inkstand NOUN an inkstand is a pot which was put on a desk to contain either ink or pencils and pens ❏ *throwing an inkstand at the Lizard as she spoke* (*Alice's Adventures in Wonderland* by Lewis Carroll)

inordinate ADJ without order. To-day inordinate means 'excessive'. ❏ *Though yet untutored and inordinate* (*The Prelude* by William Wordsworth)

intellectuals NOUN here intellectuals means the minds (of the workmen) ❏ *those instructions they give being too refined for the intellectuals of their workmen* (*Gulliver's Travels* by Jonathan Swift)

interview NOUN meeting ❏ *By our first strange and fatal interview* (*On His Mistress* by John Donne)

jacks NOUN jacks are rods for turning a spit over a fire ❏ *It was a small bit of pork suspended from the kettle hanger by a string passed through a large door key, in a way known to primitive housekeepers unpossessed of jacks* (*Silas Marner* by George Eliot)

jews-harp NOUN a jews-harp is a small, metal, musical instrument that is played by the mouth ❏ *A jews-harp's plenty good enough for a rat* (*The Adventures of Huckleberry Finn* by Mark Twain)

jorum NOUN a large bowl ❏ *while Miss Skiffins brewed such a jorum of tea, that the pig in the back premises became strongly excited* (*Great Expectations* by Charles Dickens)

jostled VERB jostled means bumped or pushed by someone or some people

❏ *being jostled himself into the kennel* (*Gulliver's Travels* by Jonathan Swift)

keepsake NOUN a keepsake is a gift which reminds someone of an event or of the person who gave it to them. ❏ *books and ornaments they had in their boudoirs at home: keepsakes that different relations had presented to them* (*Jane Eyre* by Charlotte Brontë)

kenned VERB kenned means knew ❏ *though little kenned the lamplighter that he had any company that Christmas!* (*A Christmas Carol* by Charles Dickens)

kennel NOUN kennel means gutter, which is the edge of a road next to the pavement, where rain water collects and flows away ❏ *being jostled himself into the kennel* (*Gulliver's Travels* by Jonathan Swift)

knock-knee ADJ knock-knee means slanted, at an angle. ❏ *LOT 1 was marked in whitewashed knock-knee letters on the brewhouse* (*Great Expectations* by Charles Dickens)

ladylike ADJ to be ladylike is to behave in a polite, dignified and graceful way ❏ *No, winking isn't ladylike* (*Little Women* by Louisa May Alcott)

lapse NOUN flow ❏ *Stealing with silent lapse to join the brook* (*The Prelude* by William Wordsworth)

larry NOUN larry is an old word which means commotion or noisy celebration ❏ *That was all a part of the larry!* (*Tess of the D'Urbervilles* by Thomas Hardy)

laths NOUN laths are strips of wood ❏ *The panels shrunk, the windows cracked; fragments of plaster fell out of the ceiling, and the naked laths were shown instead* (*A Christmas Carol* by Charles Dickens)

leer NOUN a leer is an unpleasant smile ❏ *with a kind of leer* (*Treasure Island* by Robert Louis Stevenson)

lenitives NOUN these are different kinds of drugs or medicines: lenitives and palliatives were pain relievers; aperitives were laxatives; abstersives caused vomiting; corrosives destroyed human tissue; restringents caused constipation; cephalalgics stopped headaches; icterics were used as medicine for jaundice; apophlegmatics were cough medicine, and acoustics were cures for the loss of hearing ❑ *lenitives, aperitives, abstersives, corrosives, restringents, palliatives, laxatives, cephalalgics, icterics, apophlegmatics, acoustics* (*Gulliver's Travels* by Jonathan Swift)

lest CONJ in case. If you do something lest something (usually) unpleasant happens you do it to try to prevent it happening ❑ *She went in without knocking, and hurried upstairs, in great fear lest she should meet the real Mary Ann* (*Alice's Adventures in Wonderland* by Lewis Carroll)

levee NOUN a levee is an old term for a meeting held in the morning, shortly after the person holding the meeting has got out of bed ❑ *I used to attend the King's levee once or twice a week* (*Gulliver's Travels* by Jonathan Swift)

life-preserver NOUN a club which had lead inside it to make it heavier and therefore more dangerous ❑ *and with no more suspicious articles displayed to view than two or three heavy bludgeons which stood in a corner, and a 'life-preserver' that hung over the chimney-piece.* (*Oliver Twist* by Charles Dickens)

lighterman NOUN a lighterman is another word for sailor ❑ *in and out, hammers going in ship-builders' yards, saws going at timber, clashing engines going at things unknown, pumps going in leaky ships, capstans going, ships going out to sea, and unintelligible sea creatures roaring curses over the bulwarks at respondent lightermen* (*Great Expectations* by Charles Dickens)

livery NOUN servants often wore a uniform known as a livery ❑

suddenly a footman in livery came running out of the wood (*Alice's Adventures in Wonderland* by Lewis Carroll)

livid ADJ livid means pale or ash coloured. Livid also means very angry ❑ *a dirty, livid white* (*Treasure Island* by Robert Louis Stevenson)

lottery-tickets NOUN a popular card game ❑ *and Mrs. Philips protested that they would have a nice comfortable noisy game of lottery tickets* (*Pride and Prejudice* by Jane Austen)

lower and upper world PHRASE the earth and the heavens are the lower and upper worlds ❑ *the changes in the lower and upper world* (*Gulliver's Travels* by Jonathan Swift)

lustres NOUN lustres are chandeliers. A chandelier is a large, decorative frame which holds light bulbs or candles and hangs from the ceiling ❑ *the lustres, lights, the carving and the guilding* (*The Prelude* by William Wordsworth)

lynched VERB killed without a criminal trial by a crowd of people ❑ *He'll never know how nigh he come to getting lynched* (*The Adventures of Huckleberry Finn* by Mark Twain)

malingering VERB if someone is malingering they are pretending to be ill to avoid working ❑ *And you stand there malingering* (*Treasure Island* by Robert Louis Stevenson)

managing PHRASE treating with consideration ❑ *to think the honour of my own kind not worth managing* (*Gulliver's Travels* by Jonathan Swift)

manhood PHRASE manhood means human nature ❑ *concerning the nature of manhood* (*Gulliver's Travels* by Jonathan Swift)

man-trap NOUN a man-trap is a set of steel jaws that snap shut when trodden on and trap a person's leg

❏ *"Don't go to him," I called out of the window, "he's an assassin! A man-trap!"* (*Oliver Twist* by Charles Dickens)

maps NOUN charts of the night sky ❏ *Let maps to others, worlds on worlds have shown* (*The Good-Morrow* by John Donne)

mark VERB look at or notice ❏ *Mark but this flea, and mark in this* (*The Flea* by John Donne)

maroons NOUN A maroon is someone who has been left in a place which it is difficult for them to escape from, like a small island ❏ *if schooners, islands, and maroons* (*Treasure Island* by Robert Louis Stevenson)

mast NOUN here mast means the fruit of forest trees ❏ *a quantity of acorns, dates, chestnuts, and other mast* (*Gulliver's Travels* by Jonathan Swift)

mate VERB defeat ❏ *Where Mars did mate the warlike Carthigens* (*Doctor Faustus Chorus* by Christopher Marlowe)

mealy ADJ Mealy when used to describe a face meant pallid, pale or colourless ❏ *I only know two sorts of boys. Mealy boys, and beef-faced boys* (*Oliver Twist* by Charles Dickens)

middling ADV fairly or moderately ❏ *she worked me middling hard for about an hour* (*The Adventures of Huckleberry Finn* by Mark Twain)

mill NOUN a mill, or treadmill, was a device for hard labour or punishment in prison ❏ *Was you never on the mill?* (*Oliver Twist* by Charles Dickens)

milliner's shop NOUN a milliner's sold fabrics, clothing, lace and accessories; as time went on they specialized more and more in hats ❏ *to pay their duty to their aunt and to a milliner's shop just over the way* (*Pride and Prejudice* by Jane Austen)

minching un' munching PHRASE how people in the north of England used to describe the way people

from the south speak ❏ *Minching un' munching!* (*Wuthering Heights* by Emily Brontë)

mine NOUN gold ❏ *Whether both th'Indias of spice and mine* (*The Sun Rising* by John Donne)

mire NOUN mud ❏ *Tis my fate to be always ground into the mire under the iron heel of oppression* (*The Adventures of Huckleberry Finn* by Mark Twain)

miscellany NOUN a miscellany is a collection of many different kinds of things ❏ *under that, the miscellany began* (*Treasure Island* by Robert Louis Stevenson)

mistarshers NOUN mistarshers means moustache, which is the hair that grows on a man's upper lip ❏ *when he put his hand up to his mistarshers* (*Tess of the D'Urbervilles* by Thomas Hardy)

morrow NOUN here good-morrow means tomorrow and a new and better life ❏ *And now good-morrow to our waking souls* (*The Good-Morrow* by John Donne)

mortification NOUN mortification is an old word for gangrene which is when part of the body decays or 'dies' because of disease ❏ *Yes, it was a mortification–that was it* (*The Adventures of Huckleberry Finn* by Mark Twain)

mought VERB mought is an old spelling of might ❏ *what you mought call me? You mought call me captain* (*Treasure Island* by Robert Louis Stevenson)

move VERB move me not means do not make me angry ❏ *Move me not, Faustus* (*Doctor Faustus 2.1* by Christopher Marlowe)

muffin-cap NOUN a muffin-cap is a flat cap made from wool ❏ *the old one, remained stationary in the muffin-cap and leathers* (*Oliver Twist* by Charles Dickens)

mulatter NOUN a mulatter was another word for mulatto, which is a person with parents who are from different races ❑ *a mulatter, most as white as a white man* (*The Adventures of Huckleberry Finn* by Mark Twain)

mummery NOUN mummery is an old word that meant meaningless (or pretentious) ceremony ❑ *When they were all gone, and when Trabb and his men—but not his boy: I looked for him—had crammed their mummery into bags, and were gone too, the house felt wholesomer.* (*Great Expectations* by Charles Dickens)

nap NOUN the nap is the woolly surface on a new item of clothing. Here the surface has been worn away so it looks bare ❑ *like an old hat with the nap rubbed off* (*The Adventures of Huckleberry Finn* by Mark Twain)

natural ■ NOUN a natural is a person born with learning difficulties ❑ *though he had been left to his particular care by their deceased father, who thought him almost a natural.* (*David Copperfield* by Charles Dickens) ■ ADJ natural meant illegitimate ❑ *Harriet Smith was the natural daughter of somebody* (*Emma* by Jane Austen)

navigator NOUN a navigator was originally someone employed to dig canals. It is the origin of the word 'navvy' meaning a labourer ❑ *She ascertained from me in a few words what it was all about, comforted Dora, and gradually convinced her that I was not a labourer—from my manner of stating the case I believe Dora concluded that I was a navigator, and went balancing myself up and down a plank all day with a wheelbarrow—and so brought us together in peace.* (*David Copperfield* by Charles Dickens)

necromancy NOUN necromancy means a kind of magic where the magician speaks to spirits or ghosts to find out what will happen in the future ❑ *He surfeits upon cursed necromancy* (*Doctor Faustus chorus* by Christopher Marlowe)

negus NOUN a negus is a hot drink made from sweetened wine and water ❑ *He sat placidly perusing the newspaper, with his little head on one side, and a glass of warm sherry negus at his elbow.* (*David Copperfield* by Charles Dickens)

nice ADJ discriminating. Able to make good judgements or choices ❑ *consequently a claim to be nice* (*Emma* by Jane Austen)

nigh ADV nigh means near ❑ *He'll never know how nigh he come to getting lynched* (*The Adventures of Huckleberry Finn* by Mark Twain)

nimbleness NOUN nimbleness means being able to move very quickly or skilfully ❑ *and with incredible accuracy and nimbleness* (*Treasure Island* by Robert Louis Stevenson)

noggin NOUN a noggin is a small mug or a wooden cup ❑ *you'll bring me one noggin of rum* (*Treasure Island* by Robert Louis Stevenson)

none ADJ neither ❑ *none can die* (*The Good-Morrow* by John Donne)

notices NOUN observations ❑ *Arch are his notices* (*The Prelude* by William Wordsworth)

occiput NOUN occiput means the back of the head ❑ *saw off the occiput of each couple* (*Gulliver's Travels* by Jonathan Swift)

officiously ADV kindly ❑ *the governess who attended Glumdalclitch very officiously lifted me up* (*Gulliver's Travels* by Jonathan Swift)

old salt PHRASE old salt is a slang term for an experienced sailor ❑ *a 'true sea-dog', and a 'real old salt'* (*Treasure Island* by Robert Louis Stevenson)

or ere PHRASE before ❑ *or ere the Hall was built* (*The Prelude* by William Wordsworth)

ostler NOUN one who looks after horses at an inn ❑ *The bill paid, and the waiter remembered, and the ostler not forgotten, and the chambermaid taken into consideration* (*Great Expectations* by Charles Dickens)

ostry NOUN an ostry is an old word for a pub or hotel ❑ *lest I send you into the ostry with a vengeance* (*Doctor Faustus 2.2* by Christopher Marlowe)

outrunning the constable PHRASE outrunning the constable meant spending more than you earn ❑ *but I shall by this means be able to check your bills and to pull you up if I find you outrunning the constable.* (*Great Expectations* by Charles Dickens)

over ADV across ❑ *It is in length six yards, and in the thickest part at least three yards over* (*Gulliver's Travels* by Jonathan Swift)

over the broomstick PHRASE this is a phrase meaning 'getting married without a formal ceremony' ❑ *They both led tramping lives, and this woman in Gerrard-street here, had been married very young, over the broomstick (as we say), to a tramping man, and was a perfect fury in point of jealousy.* (*Great Expectations* by Charles Dickens)

own VERB own means to admit or to acknowledge ❑ *It's my old girl that advises. She has the head. But I never own to it before her. Discipline must be maintained* (*Bleak House* by Charles Dickens)

page NOUN here page means a boy employed to run errands ❑ *not my feigned page* (*On His Mistress* by John Donne)

paid pretty dear PHRASE paid pretty dear means paid a high price or suffered quite a lot ❑ *I paid pretty dear for my monthly fourpenny piece* (*Treasure Island* by Robert Louis Stevenson)

pannikins NOUN pannikins were small tin cups ❑ *of lifting light glasses and cups to his lips, as if they were clumsy pannikins* (*Great Expectations* by Charles Dickens)

pards NOUN pards are leopards ❑ *Not charioted by Bacchus and his pards* (*Ode on a Nightingale* by John Keats)

parlour boarder NOUN a pupil who lived with the family ❑ *and somebody had lately raised her from the condition of scholar to parlour boarder* (*Emma* by Jane Austen)

particular, a London PHRASE London in Victorian times and up to the 1950s was famous for having very dense fog–which was a combination of real fog and the smog of pollution from factories ❑ *This is a London particular . . . A fog, miss* (*Bleak House* by Charles Dickens)

patten NOUN pattens were wooden soles which were fixed to shoes by straps to protect the shoes in wet weather ❑ *carrying a basket like the Great Seal of England in plaited straw, a pair of pattens, a spare shawl, and an umbrella, though it was a fine bright day* (*Great Expectations* by Charles Dickens)

paviour NOUN a paviour was a labourer who worked on the street pavement ❑ *the paviour his pickaxe* (*Oliver Twist* by Charles Dickens)

peccant ADJ peccant means unhealthy ❑ *other peccant humours* (*Gulliver's Travels* by Jonathan Swift)

penetralium NOUN penetralium is a word used to describe the inner rooms of the house ❑ *and I had no desire to aggravate his impatience previous to inspecting the penetralium* (*Wuthering Heights* by Emily Brontë)

pensive ADV pensive means deep in thought or thinking seriously about something ❑ *and she was leaning pensive on a tomb-stone on her right elbow* (*The Adventures of Huckleberry Finn* by Mark Twain)

penury NOUN penury is the state of being extremely poor ❑ *Distress, if not penury, loomed in the distance* (*Tess of the D'Urbervilles* by Thomas Hardy)

perspective NOUN telescope ❑ *a pocket perspective* (*Gulliver's Travels* by Jonathan Swift)

phaeton NOUN a phaeton was an open carriage for four people ❑ *often* *condescends to drive by my humble abode in her little phaeton and ponies* (Pride and Prejudice by Jane Austen)

phantasm NOUN a phantasm is an illusion, something that is not real. It is sometimes used to mean ghost ❑ *Experience had bred no fancies in him that could raise the phantasm of appetite* (Silas Marner by George Eliot)

physic NOUN here physic means medicine ❑ *there I studied physic two years and seven months* (Gulliver's Travels by Jonathan Swift)

pinioned VERB to pinion is to hold both arms so that a person cannot move them ❑ *But the relentless Ghost pinioned him in both his arms, and forced him to observe what happened next.* (A Christmas Carol by Charles Dickens)

piquet NOUN piquet was a popular card game in the C18th ❑ *Mr Hurst and Mr Bingley were at piquet* (Pride and Prejudice by Jane Austen)

plaister NOUN a plaister is a piece of cloth on which an apothecary (or pharmacist) would spread ointment. The cloth is then applied to wounds or bruises to treat them ❑ *Then, she gave the knife a final smart wipe on the edge of the plaister, and then sawed a very thick round off the loaf: which she finally, before separating from the loaf, hewed into two halves, of which Joe got one, and I the other.* (Great Expectations by Charles Dickens)

plantations NOUN here plantations means colonies, which are countries controlled by a more powerful country ❑ *besides our plantations in America* (Gulliver's Travels by Jonathan Swift)

plastic ADJ here plastic is an old term meaning shaping or a power that was forming ❑ *A plastic power abode with me* (The Prelude by William Wordsworth)

players NOUN actors ❑ *of players which upon the world's stage be* (On His Mistress by John Donne)

plump ADV all at once, suddenly ❑ *But it took a bit of time to get it well round, the change come so uncommon plump, didn't it?* (Great Expectations by Charles Dickens)

plundered VERB to plunder is to rob or steal from ❑ *These crosses stand for the names of ships or towns that they sank or plundered* (Treasure Island by Robert Louis Stevenson)

pommel ■ VERB to pommel someone is to hit them repeatedly with your fists ❑ *hug him round the neck, pommel his back, and kick his legs in irrepressible affection!* (A Christmas Carol by Charles Dickens) ■ NOUN a pommel is the part of a saddle that rises up at the front ❑ *He had his gun across his pommel* (The Adventures of Huckleberry Finn by Mark Twain)

poor's rates NOUN poor's rates were property taxes which were used to support the poor ❑ *"Oh!" replied the undertaker; "why, you know, Mr. Bumble, I pay a good deal towards the poor's rates."* (Oliver Twist by Charles Dickens)

popular ADJ popular means ruled by the people, or Republican, rather than ruled by a monarch ❑ *With those of Greece compared and popular Rome* (The Prelude by William Wordsworth)

porringer NOUN a porringer is a small bowl ❑ *Of this festive composition each boy had one porringer, and no more* (Oliver Twist by Charles Dickens)

postboy NOUN a postboy was the driver of a horse-drawn carriage ❑ *He spoke to a postboy who was dozing under the gateway* (Oliver Twist by Charles Dickens)

post-chaise NOUN a fast carriage for two or four passengers ❑ *Looking round, he saw that it was a post-chaise, driven at great speed* (Oliver Twist by Charles Dickens)

postern NOUN a small gate usually at the back of a building ❑ *The little servant happening to be entering the* fortress with two hot rolls, I passed through the postern and crossed the drawbridge, in her company (*Great Expectations* by Charles Dickens)

pottle NOUN a pottle was a small basket ❑ *He had a paper-bag under each arm and a pottle of strawberries in one hand . . .* (*Great Expectations* by Charles Dickens)

pounce NOUN pounce is a fine powder used to prevent ink spreading on untreated paper ❑ *in that grim atmosphere of pounce and parchment, red-tape, dusty wafers, ink-jars, brief and draft paper, law reports, writs, declarations, and bills of costs* (*David Copperfield* by Charles Dickens)

pox NOUN pox means sexually transmitted diseases like syphilis ❑ *how the pox in all its consequences and denominations* (*Gulliver's Travels* by Jonathan Swift)

prelibation NOUN prelibation means a foretaste of or an example of something to come ❑ *A prelibation to the mower's scythe* (*The Prelude* by William Wordsworth)

prentice NOUN an apprentice ❑ *and Joe, sitting on an old gun, had told me that when I was 'prentice to him regularly bound, we would have such Larks there!* (*Great Expectations* by Charles Dickens)

presently ADV immediately ❑ *I presently knew what they meant* (*Gulliver's Travels* by Jonathan Swift)

pumpion NOUN pumpkin ❑ *for it was almost as large as a small pumpion* (*Gulliver's Travels* by Jonathan Swift)

punctual ADJ kept in one place ❑ *was not a punctual presence, but a spirit* (*The Prelude* by William Wordsworth)

quadrille ■ NOUN a quadrille is a dance invented in France which is usually performed by four couples ❑ *However, Mr Swiveller had Miss Sophy's hand for the first quadrille (country-dances being low, were utterly proscribed)* (*The Old Curiosity Shop* by Charles Dickens) ■ NOUN quadrille was a card game for four people ❑ *to make up her pool of quadrille in the evening* (*Pride and Prejudice* by Jane Austen)

quality NOUN gentry or upper-class people ❑ *if you are with the quality* (*The Adventures of Huckleberry Finn* by Mark Twain)

quick parts PHRASE quick-witted ❑ *Mr Bennet was so odd a mixture of quick parts* (*Pride and Prejudice* by Jane Austen)

quid NOUN a quid is something chewed or kept in the mouth, like a piece of tobacco ❑ *rolling his quid* (*Treasure Island* by Robert Louis Stevenson)

quit VERB quit means to avenge or to make even ❑ *But Faustus's death shall quit my infamy* (*Doctor Faustus 4.3* by Christopher Marlowe)

rags NOUN divisions ❑ *Nor hours, days, months, which are the rags of time* (*The Sun Rising* by John Donne)

raiment NOUN raiment means clothing ❑ *the mountain shook off turf and flower, had only heath for raiment and crag for gem* (*Jane Eyre* by Charlotte Brontë)

rain cats and dogs PHRASE an expression meaning rain heavily. The origin of the expression is unclear ❑ *But it'll perhaps rain cats and dogs to-morrow* (*Silas Marner* by George Eliot)

raised Cain PHRASE raised Cain means caused a lot of trouble. Cain is a character in the Bible who killed his brother Abel ❑ *and every time he got drunk he raised Cain around town* (*The Adventures of Huckleberry Finn* by Mark Twain)

rambling ADJ rambling means confused and not very clear ❑ *my head began to be filled very early with rambling thoughts* (*Robinson Crusoe* by Daniel Defoe)

raree-show NOUN a raree-show is an old term for a peep-show or a fairground entertainment ❑ *A raree-show is here, with children gathered round* (*The Prelude* by William Wordsworth)

recusants NOUN people who resisted authority ❑ *hardy recusants* (*The Prelude* by William Wordsworth)

redounding VERB eddying. An eddy is a movement in water or air which goes round and round instead of flowing in one direction ❑ *mists and steam-like fogs redounding everywhere* (*The Prelude* by William Wordsworth)

redundant ADJ here redundant means overflowing but Wordsworth also uses it to mean excessively large or too big ❑ *A tempest, a redundant energy* (*The Prelude* by William Wordsworth)

reflex NOUN reflex is a shortened version of reflexion, which is an alternative spelling of reflection ❑ *To cut across the reflex of a star* (*The Prelude* by William Wordsworth)

Reformatory NOUN a prison for young offenders/criminals ❑ *Even when I was taken to have a new suit of clothes, the tailor had orders to make them like a kind of Reformatory, and on no account to let me have the free use of my limbs.* (*Great Expectations* by Charles Dickens)

remorse NOUN pity or compassion ❑ *by that remorse* (*On His Mistress* by John Donne)

render VERB in this context render means give. ❑ *and Sarah could render no reason that would be sanctioned by the feeling of the community.* (*Silas Marner* by George Eliot)

repeater NOUN a repeater was a watch that chimed the last hour when a button was pressed—as a result it was useful in the dark ❑ *And his watch is a gold repeater, and worth a hundred pound if it's worth a penny.* (*Great Expectations* by Charles Dickens)

repugnance NOUN repugnance means a strong dislike of something or someone ❑ *overcoming a strong repugnance* (*Treasure Island* by Robert Louis Stevenson)

reverence NOUN reverence means bow. When you bow to someone, you briefly bend your body towards them as a formal way of showing them respect ❑ *made my reverence* (*Gulliver's Travels* by Jonathan Swift)

reverie NOUN a reverie is a daydream ❑ *I can guess the subject of your reverie* (*Pride and Prejudice* by Jane Austen)

revival NOUN a religious meeting held in public ❑ *well I'd ben a-running' a little temperance revival thar' bout a week* (*The Adventures of Huckleberry Finn* by Mark Twain)

revolt VERB revolt means turn back or stop your present course of action and go back to what you were doing before ❑ *Revolt, or I'll in piecemeal tear thy flesh* (*Doctor Faustus 5.1* by Christopher Marlowe)

rheumatics/rheumatism NOUN rheumatics [rheumatism] is an illness that makes your joints or muscles stiff and painful ❑ *a new cure for the rheumatics* (*Treasure Island* by Robert Louis Stevenson)

riddance NOUN riddance is usually used in the form good riddance which you say when you are pleased that something has gone or been left behind ❑ *I'd better go into the house, and die and be a riddance* (*David Copperfield* by Charles Dickens)

rimy ADJ rimy is an adjective which means covered in ice or frost ❑ *It was a rimy morning, and very damp* (*Great Expectations* by Charles Dickens)

riper ADJ riper means more mature or older ❑ *At riper years to Wittenberg he went* (*Doctor Faustus chorus* by Christopher Marlowe)

rubber NOUN a set of games in whist or backgammon ❏ *her father was sure of his rubber* (*Emma* by Jane Austen)

ruffian NOUN a ruffian is a person who behaves violently ❏ *and when the ruffian had told him* (*Treasure Island* by Robert Louis Stevenson)

sadness NOUN sadness is an old term meaning seriousness ❏ *But I prithee tell me, in good sadness* (*Doctor Faustus 2.2* by Christopher Marlowe)

sailed before the mast PHRASE this phrase meant someone who did not look like a sailor ❏ *he had none of the appearance of a man that sailed before the mast* (*Treasure Island* by Robert Louis Stevenson)

scabbard NOUN a scabbard is the covering for a sword or dagger ❏ *Girded round its middle was an antique scabbard; but no sword was in it, and the ancient sheath was eaten up with rust* (*A Christmas Carol* by Charles Dickens)

schooners NOUN A schooner is a fast, medium-sized sailing ship ❏ *if schooners, islands, and maroons* (*Treasure Island* by Robert Louis Stevenson)

science NOUN learning or knowledge ❏ *Even Science, too, at hand* (*The Prelude* by William Wordsworth)

scrouge VERB to scrouge means to squeeze or to crowd ❏ *to scrouge in and get a sight* (*The Adventures of Huckleberry Finn* by Mark Twain)

scrutore NOUN a scrutore, or escritoire, was a writing table ❏ *set me gently on my feet upon the scrutore* (*Gulliver's Travels* by Jonathan Swift)

scutcheon/escutcheon NOUN an escutcheon is a shield with a coat of arms, or the symbols of a family name, engraved on it ❏ *On the scutcheon we'll have a bend* (*The Adventures of Huckleberry Finn* by Mark Twain)

sea-dog PHRASE sea-dog is a slang term for an experienced sailor or pirate ❏ *a 'true sea-dog', and a 'real old salt,'* (*Treasure Island* by Robert Louis Stevenson)

see the lions PHRASE to see the lions was to go and see the sights of London. Originally the phrase referred to the menagerie in the Tower of London and later in Regent's Park ❏ *We will go and see the lions for an hour or two–it's something to have a fresh fellow like you to show them to, Copperfield* (*David Copperfield* by Charles Dickens)

self-conceit NOUN self-conceit is an old term which means having too high an opinion of oneself, or deceiving yourself ❏ *Till swollen with cunning, of a self-conceit* (*Doctor Faustus chorus* by Christopher Marlowe)

seneschal NOUN a steward ❏ *where a grey-headed seneschal sings a funny chorus with a funnier body of vassals* (*Oliver Twist* by Charles Dickens)

sensible ADJ if you were sensible of something you are aware or conscious of something ❏ *If my children are silly I must hope to be always sensible of it* (*Pride and Prejudice* by Jane Austen)

sessions NOUN court cases were heard at specific times of the year called sessions ❏ *He lay in prison very ill, during the whole interval between his committal for trial, and the coming round of the Sessions.* (*Great Expectations* by Charles Dickens)

shabby ADJ shabby places look old and in bad condition ❏ *a little bit of a shabby village named Pikesville* (*The Adventures of Huckleberry Finn* by Mark Twain)

shay-cart NOUN a shay-cart was a small cart drawn by one horse ❏ *"I were at the Bargemen t'other night, Pip;" whenever he subsided into affection, he called me Pip, and whenever he relapsed into politeness he called me Sir; "when there come up in his* *shay-cart Pumblechook." (Great Expectations* by Charles Dickens)

shilling NOUN a shilling is an old unit of currency. There were twenty shillings in every British pound ❑ *"Ten shillings too much," said the gentleman in the white waistcoat.* (*Oliver Twist* by Charles Dickens)

shines NOUN tricks or games ❑ *well, it would make a cow laugh to see the shines that old idiot cut* (*The Adventures of Huckleberry Finn* by Mark Twain)

shirking VERB shirking means not doing what you are meant to be doing, or evading your duties ❑ *some of you shirking lubbers* (*Treasure Island* by Robert Louis Stevenson)

shiver my timbers PHRASE shiver my timbers is an expression which was used by sailors and pirates to express surprise ❑ *why, shiver my timbers, if I hadn't forgotten my score!* (*Treasure Island* by Robert Louis Stevenson)

shoe-roses NOUN shoe-roses were roses made from ribbons which were stuck on to shoes as decoration ❑ *the very shoe-roses for Netherfield were got by proxy* (*Pride and Prejudice* by Jane Austen)

singular ADJ singular means very great and remarkable or strange ❑ *"Singular dream," he says* (*The Adventures of Huckleberry Finn* by Mark Twain)

sire NOUN sire is an old word which means lord or master or elder ❑ *She also defied her sire* (*Little Women* by Louisa May Alcott)

sixpence NOUN a sixpence was half of a shilling ❑ *if she had only a shilling in the world, she would be very lilkely to give away sixpence of it* (*Emma* by Jane Austen)

slavey NOUN the word slavey was used when there was only one servant in a house or boarding-house—so she had to perform all the duties of a larger staff ❑ *Two distinct knocks, sir, will produce the slavey at any*

time (*The Old Curiosity Shop* by Charles Dickens)

slender ADJ weak ❑ *In slender accents of sweet verse* (*The Prelude* by William Wordsworth)

slop-shops NOUN slop-shops were shops where cheap ready-made clothes were sold. They mainly sold clothes to sailors ❑ *Accordingly, I took the jacket off, that I might learn to do without it; and carrying it under my arm, began a tour of inspection of the various slop-shops.* (*David Copperfield* by Charles Dickens)

sluggard NOUN a lazy person ❑ *"Stand up and repeat 'Tis the voice of the sluggard,'" said the Gryphon.* (*Alice's Adventures in Wonderland* by Lewis Carroll)

smallpox NOUN smallpox is a serious infectious disease ❑ *by telling the men we had smallpox aboard* (*The Adventures of Huckleberry Finn* by Mark Twain)

smalls NOUN smalls are short trousers ❑ *It is difficult for a large-headed, small-eyed youth, of lumbering make and heavy countenance, to look dignified under any circumstances; but it is more especially so, when superadded to these personal attractions are a red nose and yellow smalls* (*Oliver Twist* by Charles Dickens)

sneeze-box NOUN a box for snuff was called a sneeze-box because sniffing snuff makes the user sneeze ❑ *To think of Jack Dawkins — lummy Jack — the Dodger — the Artful Dodger — going abroad for a common twopenny-halfpenny sneeze-box!* (*Oliver Twist* by Charles Dickens)

snorted VERB slept ❑ *Or snorted we in the Seven Sleepers' den?* (*The Good-Morrow* by John Donne)

snuff NOUN snuff is tobacco in powder form which is taken by sniffing ❑ *as he thrust his thumb and forefinger into the proffered snuff-box of the undertaker: which was an* ingenious little model of a patent coffin. (*Oliver Twist* by Charles Dickens)

soliloquized VERB to soliloquize is when an actor in a play speaks to himself or herself rather than to another actor ❑ *"A new servitude! There is something in that," I soliloquized (mentally, be it understood; I did not talk aloud)* (*Jane Eyre* by Charlotte Brontë)

sough NOUN a sough is a drain or a ditch ❑ *as you may have noticed the sough that runs from the marshes* (*Wuthering Heights* by Emily Brontë)

spirits NOUN a spirit is the nonphysical part of a person which is believed to remain alive after their death ❑ *that I might raise up spirits when I please* (*Doctor Faustus* 1.5 by Christopher Marlowe)

spleen ■ NOUN here spleen means a type of sadness or depression which was thought to only affect the wealthy ❑ *yet here I could plainly discover the true seeds of spleen* (*Gulliver's Travels* by Jonathan Swift) ■ NOUN irritability and low spirits ❑ *Adieu to disappointment and spleen* (*Pride and Prejudice* by Jane Austen)

spondulicks NOUN spondulicks is a slang word which means money ❑ *not for all his spondulicks and as much more on top of it* (*The Adventures of Huckleberry Finn* by Mark Twain)

stalled of VERB to be stalled of something is to be bored with it ❑ *I'm stalled of doing naught* (*Wuthering Heights* by Emily Brontë)

stanchion NOUN a stanchion is a pole or bar that stands upright and is used as a building support ❑ *and slid down a stanchion* (*The Adventures of Huckleberry Finn* by Mark Twain)

stang NOUN stang is another word for pole which was an old measurement ❑ *These fields were intermingled with woods of half a stang* (*Gulliver's Travels* by Jonathan Swift)

starlings NOUN a starling is a wall built around the pillars that support a bridge to protect the pillars ❑ *There were states of the tide when, having been down the river, I could not get back through the eddy-chafed arches and starlings of old London Bridge* (*Great Expectations* by Charles Dickens)

startings NOUN twitching or night-time movements of the body ❑ *with midnight's startings* (*On His Mistress* by John Donne)

stomacher NOUN a panel at the front of a dress ❑ *but send her aunt the pattern of a stomacher* (*Emma* by Jane Austen)

stoop VERB swoop ❑ *Once a kite hovering over the garden made a stoop at me* (*Gulliver's Travels* by Jonathan Swift)

succedaneum NOUN a succedaneum is a substitute ❑ *But as a succedaneum* (*The Prelude* by William Wordsworth)

suet NOUN a hard animal fat used in cooking ❑ *and your jaws are too weak For anything tougher than suet* (*Alice's Adventures in Wonderland* by Lewis Carroll)

sultry ADJ sultry weather is hot and damp. Here sultry means unpleasant or risky ❑ *for it was getting pretty sultry for us* (*The Adventures of Huckleberry Finn* by Mark Twain)

summerset NOUN summerset is an old spelling of somersault. If someone does a somersault, they turn over completely in the air ❑ *I have seen him do the summerset* (*Gulliver's Travels* by Jonathan Swift)

supper NOUN supper was a light meal taken late in the evening. The main meal was dinner which was eaten at four or five in the afternoon ❑ *and the supper table was all set out* (*Emma* by Jane Austen)

surfeits VERB to surfeit in something is to have far too much of it, or to overindulge in it to an unhealthy degree ❑ *He surfeits upon cursed* necromancy (*Doctor Faustus chorus* by Christopher Marlowe)

surtout NOUN a surtout is a long close-fitting overcoat ❑ *He wore a long black surtout reaching nearly to his ankles* (*The Old Curiosity Shop* by Charles Dickens)

swath NOUN swath is the width of corn cut by a scythe ❑ *while thy hook Spares the next swath* (*Ode to Autumn* by John Keats)

sylvan ADJ sylvan means belonging to the woods ❑ *Sylvan historian* (*Ode on a Grecian Urn* by John Keats)

taction NOUN taction means touch. This means that the people had to be touched on the mouth or the ears to get their attention ❑ *without being roused by some external taction upon the organs of speech and hearing* (*Gulliver's Travels* by Jonathan Swift)

Tag and Rag and Bobtail PHRASE the riff-raff, or lower classes. Used in an insulting way ❑ *"No," said he; "not till it got about that there was no protection on the premises, and it come to be considered dangerous, with convicts and Tag and Rag and Bobtail going up and down."* (*Great Expectations* by Charles Dickens)

tallow NOUN tallow is hard animal fat that is used to make candles and soap ❑ *and a lot of tallow candles* (*The Adventures of Huckleberry Finn* by Mark Twain)

tan VERB to tan means to beat or whip ❑ *and if I catch you about that school I'll tan you good* (*The Adventures of Huckleberry Finn* by Mark Twain)

tanyard NOUN the tanyard is part of a tannery, which is a place where leather is made from animal skins ❑ *hid in the old tanyard* (*The Adventures of Huckleberry Finn* by Mark Twain)

tarry ADJ tarry means the colour of tar or black ❑ *his tarry pig-tail*

(*Treasure Island* by Robert Louis Stevenson)

thereof PHRASE from there ❑ *By all desires which thereof did ensue* (*On His Mistress* by John Donne)

thick with, be PHRASE if you are "thick with someone" you are very close, sharing secrets–it is often used to describe people who are planning something secret ❑ *Hasn't he been thick with Mr Heathcliff lately?* (*Wuthering Heights* by Emily Brontë)

thimble NOUN a thimble is a small cover used to protect the finger while sewing ❑ *The paper had been sealed in several places by a thimble* (*Treasure Island* by Robert Louis Stevenson)

thirtover ADJ thirtover is an old word which means obstinate or that someone is very determined to do want they want and can not be persuaded to do something in another way ❑ *I have been living on in a thirtover, lackadaisical way* (*Tess of the D'Urbervilles* by Thomas Hardy)

timbrel NOUN timbrel is a tambourine ❑ *What pipes and timbrels?* (*Ode on a Grecian Urn* by John Keats)

tin NOUN tin is slang for money/cash ❑ *Then the plain question is, an't it a pity that this state of things should continue, and how much better would it be for the old gentleman to hand over a reasonable amount of tin, and make it all right and comfortable* (*The Old Curiosity Shop* by Charles Dickens)

tincture NOUN a tincture is a medicine made with alcohol and a small amount of a drug ❑ *with ink composed of a cephalic tincture* (*Gulliver's Travels* by Jonathan Swift)

tithe NOUN a tithe is a tax paid to the church ❑ *and held farms which, speaking from a spiritual point of view, paid highly-desirable tithes* (*Silas Marner* by George Eliot)

towardly ADJ a towardly child is

dutiful or obedient ❑ *and a towardly child* (*Gulliver's Travels* by Jonathan Swift)

toys NOUN trifles are things which are considered to have little importance, value, or significance ❑ *purchase my life from them bysome bracelets, glass rings, and other toys* (*Gulliver's Travels* by Jonathan Swift)

tract NOUN a tract is a religious pamphlet or leaflet ❑ *and Joe Harper got a hymn-book and a tract* (*The Adventures of Huckleberry Finn* by Mark Twain)

train-oil NOUN train-oil is oil from whale blubber ❑ *The train-oil and gunpowder were shoved out of sight in a minute* (*Wuthering Heights* by Emily Brontë)

tribulation NOUN tribulation means the suffering or difficulty you experience in a particular situation ❑ *Amy was learning this distinction through much tribulation* (*Little Women* by Louisa May Alcott)

trivet NOUN a trivet is a three-legged stand for resting a pot or kettle ❑ *a pocket-knife in his right; and a pewter pot on the trivet* (*Oliver Twist* by Charles Dickens)

trot line NOUN a trot line is a fishing line to which a row of smaller fishing lines are attached ❑ *when he got along I was hard at it taking up a trot line* (*The Adventures of Huckleberry Finn* by Mark Twain)

troth NOUN oath or pledge ❑ *I wonder, by my troth* (*The Good-Morrow* by John Donne)

truckle NOUN a truckle bedstead is a bed that is on wheels and can be slid under another bed to save space ❑ *It rose under my hand, and the door yielded. Looking in, I saw a lighted candle on a table, a bench, and a mattress on a truckle bedstead.* (*Great Expectations* by Charles Dickens)

trump NOUN a trump is a good, reliable person who can be trusted ❑ *This lad Hawkins is a trump, I perceive* (*Treasure Island* by Robert Louis Stevenson)

tucker NOUN a tucker is a frilly lace collar which is worn around the neck ❑ *Whereat Scrooge's niece's sister—the plump one with the lace tucker: not the one with the roses—blushed.* (*A Christmas Carol* by Charles Dickens)

tureen NOUN a large bowl with a lid from which soup or vegetables are served ❑ *Waiting in a hot tureen!* (*Alice's Adventures in Wonderland* by Lewis Carroll)

turnkey NOUN a prison officer; jailer ❑ *As we came out of the prison through the lodge, I found that the great importance of my guardian was appreciated by the turnkeys, no less than by those whom they held in charge.* (*Great Expectations* by Charles Dickens)

turnpike NOUN the upkeep of many roads of the time was paid for by tolls (fees) collected at posts along the road. There was a gate to prevent people travelling further along the road until the toll had been paid. ❑ *Traddles, whom I have taken up by appointment at the turnpike, presents a dazzling combination of cream colour and light blue; and both he and Mr. Dick have a general effect about them of being all gloves.* (*David Copperfield* by Charles Dickens)

twas PHRASE it was ❑ *twas but a dream of thee* (*The Good-Morrow* by John Donne)

tyrannized VERB tyrannized means bullied or forced to do things against their will ❑ *for people would soon cease coming there to be tyrannized over and put down* (*Treasure Island* by Robert Louis Stevenson)

'un NOUN 'un is a slang term for one–usually used to refer to a person ❑ *She's been thinking the old 'un* (*David Copperfield* by Charles Dickens)

undistinguished ADJ undiscriminating or incapable of making a distinction between good and bad things ❑

their undistinguished appetite to devour everything (*Gulliver's Travels* by Jonathan Swift)

use NOUN habit ❑ *Though use make you apt to kill me* (*The Flea* by John Donne)

vacant ADJ vacant usually means empty, but here Wordsworth uses it to mean carefree ❑ *To vacant musing, unreproved neglect* (*The Prelude* by William Wordsworth)

valetudinarian NOUN one too concerned with his or her own health. ❑ *for having been a valetudinarian all his life* (*Emma* by Jane Austen)

vamp VERB vamp means to walk or tramp to somewhere ❑ *Well, vamp on to Marlott, will 'ee* (*Tess of the D'Urbervilles* by Thomas Hardy)

vapours NOUN the vapours is an old term which means unpleasant and strange thoughts, which make the person feel nervous and unhappy ❑ *and my head was full of vapours* (*Robinson Crusoe* by Daniel Defoe)

vegetables NOUN here vegetables means plants ❑ *the other vegetables are in the same proportion* (*Gulliver's Travels* by Jonathan Swift)

venturesome ADJ if you are venturesome you are willing to take risks ❑ *he must be either hopelessly stupid or a venturesome fool* (*Wuthering Heights* by Emily Brontë)

verily ADV verily means really or truly ❑ *though I believe verily* (*Robinson Crusoe* by Daniel Defoe)

vicinage NOUN vicinage is an area or the residents of an area ❑ *and to his thought the whole vicinage was haunted by her.* (*Silas Marner* by George Eliot)

victuals NOUN victuals means food ❑ *grumble a little over the victuals* (*The Adventures of Huckleberry Finn* by Mark Twain)

vintage NOUN vintage in this context means wine ❑ *Oh, for a draught of*

vintage! (*Ode on a Nightingale* by John Keats)

virtual ADJ here virtual means powerful or strong ❑ *had virtual faith* (*The Prelude* by William Wordsworth)

vittles NOUN vittles is a slang word which means food ❑ *There never was such a woman for givin' away vittles and drink* (*Little Women* by Louisa May Alcott)

voided straight PHRASE voided straight is an old expression which means emptied immediately ❑ *see the rooms be voided straight* (*Doctor Faustus 4.1* by Christopher Marlowe)

wainscot NOUN wainscot is wood panel lining in a room so wainscoted means a room lined with wooden panels ❑ *in the dark wainscoted parlor* (*Silas Marner* by George Eliot)

walking the plank PHRASE walking the plank was a punishment in which a prisoner would be made to walk along a plank on the side of the ship and fall into the sea, where they would be abandoned ❑ *about hanging, and walking the plank* (*Treasure Island* by Robert Louis Stevenson)

want VERB want means to be lacking or short of ❑ *The next thing wanted was to get the picture framed* (*Emma* by Jane Austen)

wanting ADJ wanting means lacking or missing ❑ *wanting two fingers of the left hand* (*Treasure Island* by Robert Louis Stevenson)

wanting, I was not PHRASE I was not wanting means I did not fail ❑ *I was not wanting to lay a foundation of religious knowledge in his mind* (*Robinson Crusoe* by Daniel Defoe)

ward NOUN a ward is, usually, a child who has been put under the protection of the court or a guardian for his or her protection ❑ *I call the Wards in Jarndcye. The* are caged up with all the others. (*Bleak House* by Charles Dickens)

waylay VERB to waylay someone is to lie in wait for them or to intercept them ❑ *I must go up the road and waylay him* (*The Adventures of Huckleberry Finn* by Mark Twain)

weazen NOUN weazen is a slang word for throat. It actually means shrivelled ❑ *You with a uncle too! Why, I knowed you at Gargery's when you was so small a wolf that I could have took your weazen betwixt this finger and thumb and chucked you away dead* (*Great Expectations* by Charles Dickens)

wery ■ ADV very ❑ *Be wery careful o' vidders all your life* (*Pickwick Papers* by Charles Dickens) ■ *See* wibrated

wherry NOUN wherry is a small swift rowing boat for one person ❑ *It was flood tide when Daniel Quilp sat himself down in the wherry to cross to the opposite shore.* (*The Old Curiosity Shop* by Charles Dickens)

whether PREP whether means which of the two in this example ❑ *we came in full view of a great island or continent (for we knew not whether)* (*Gulliver's Travels* by Jonathan Swift)

whetstone NOUN a whetstone is a stone used to sharpen knives and other tools ❑ *I dropped pap's whetstone there too* (*The Adventures of Huckleberry Finn* by Mark Twain)

wibrated VERB in Dickens's use of the English language 'w' often replaces 'v' when he is reporting speech. So here 'wibrated' means 'vibrated'. In *Pickwick Papers* a judge asks Sam Weller (who constantly confuses the two letters) 'Do you spell it with a "v" or a "w"?' to which Weller replies 'That depends upon the taste and fancy of the speller, my Lord' ❑ *There are strings . . . in the human heart that had better not be wibrated* (*Barnaby Rudge* by Charles Dickens)

wicket NOUN a wicket is a little door in a larger entrance ❑ *Having rested here, for a minute or so, to collect a good burst of sobs and an imposing show of tears and terror, he knocked loudly at the wicket* (*Oliver Twist* by Charles Dickens)

without CONJ without means unless ❑ *You don't know about me, without you have read a book by the name of The Adventures of Tom Sawyer* (*The Adventures of Huckleberry Finn* by Mark Twain)

wittles ■ NOUN vittles is a slang word which means food ❑ *I live on broken wittles–and I sleep on the coals* (*David Copperfield* by Charles Dickens) ■ *See* wibrated

woo VERB courts or forms a proper relationship with ❑ *before it woo* (*The Flea* by John Donne)

words, to have PHRASE if you have words with someone you have a disagreement or an argument ❑ *I do not want to have words with a young thing like you.* (*Black Beauty* by Anna Sewell)

workhouse NOUN workhouses were places where the homeless were given food and a place to live in return for doing very hard work ❑ *And the Union workhouses? demanded Scrooge. Are they still in operation?* (*A Christmas Carol* by Charles Dickens)

yawl NOUN a yawl is a small boat kept on a bigger boat for short trips. Yawl is also the name for a small fishing boat ❑ *She sent out her yawl, and we went aboard* (*The Adventures of Huckleberry Finn* by Mark Twain)

yeomanry NOUN the yeomanry was a collective term for the middle classes involved in agriculture ❑ *The yeomanry are precisely the order of people with whom I feel I can have nothing to do* (*Emma* by Jane Austen)

yonder ADV yonder means over there ❑ *all in the same second we seem to hear low voices in yonder!* (*The Adventures of Huckleberry Finn* by Mark Twain)